Praise for Mandy Johnson's
Winning the War for Talent

WINNING THE WAR FOR TALENT

WINNING THE WAR FOR TALENT

How to Attract & Keep the People Who
Make Your Business Profitable

MANDY JOHNSON

WILEY

First published in 2014 by John Wiley & Sons Australia, Ltd
42 McDougall St, Milton Qld 4064

Office also in Melbourne

Typeset in 12/14.5 Bembo Std Regular

National Library of Australia Cataloguing-in-Publication data:

Author:	Johnson, Mandy, author.
Title:	Winning the War for Talent : how to attract and keep the people who make your business profitable / Mandy Johnson.
ISBN:	9780730311553 (pbk)
	9780730311560 (ebook)
Notes:	Includes index.
Subjects:	Employee retention.
	Personnel management.
	Success in business.
	Employees–Recruiting.
	Employee selection.
	Corporate culture.
	Leadership.
Dewey Number:	658.3

Cover design by Xou Creative, www.xou.com.au

Printed in Singapore by C.O.S. Printers Pte Ltd

10 9 8 7 6 5 4 3 2 1

Disclaimer
The material in this publication is of the nature of general comment only, and does not represent professional advice. It is not intended to provide specific guidance for particular circumstances and it should not be relied on as the basis for any decision to take action or not take action on any matter which it covers. Readers should obtain professional advice where appropriate, before making any such decision. To the maximum extent permitted by law, the author and publisher disclaim all responsibility and liability to any person, arising directly or indirectly from any person taking or not taking action based on the information in this publication.

All examples used throughout this book are based on real events. I have, however, changed the names of the people involved to protect both the innocent and the guilty.

Contents

About the author

Mandy Johnson is a best-selling author, the former UK Director and Australian Head of Human Resources at Flight Centre Limited (the 15 000 employee global travel retailer) and an active speaker and adviser to both public and private organisations. This book evolved from her 'Winning the War for Talent' seminar, which was Bond University's highest-rated executive education program of its year. The seminar's innovative ideas have featured in interviews in the *Australian Financial Review (AFR)* and Mandy has also spoken on radio including ABC's *Mornings with Jon Faine* and *The Conversation Hour*. She has presented business seminars in Australasia, the UK, Europe, South Africa, USA and China, and her first book *Family Village Tribe* is now studied in many MBA courses around Australia.

Mandy began her work-life as a tour leader, roving the world for three years after completing a journalism degree. On her return to Australia she joined Flight Centre where she managed several stores, started up the company's first recruitment and training centre and co-founded its UK operation, becoming the organisation's youngest ever director at the age of 28. On her return to Australia she became HR Leader and it was here, while researching a best-practice people management system, that she became an active campaigner for innovations in this field.

Dubbed 'an author HR professionals should take notice of' by *HR Magazine*, Mandy has tested her practical strategies in a diverse range of organisations, including a stint undercover in a yachting company which became an *AFR* news story. She began writing business books to share her knowledge beyond the confines of expensive seminars and consultancies and to demonstrate that great people-management is the heart, soul *and balance sheet* of every company. Mandy now lives in Queensland with her husband and two children and challenges conventional HR thinking at every opportunity.

Acknowledgements

This book wasn't a solo effort so I'd like to thank the following people who helped make it a reality: Bond University's Centre for Executive Education head, James Carlopio, who first suggested to me that my seminar 'Winning the War for Talent' was really a book in the making; Flight Centre Managing Director Graham 'Skroo' Turner and Michael Hill International CEO Mike Parsell whose encouraging comments after reading the draft manuscript kept me plugging away at it; Kristen Hammond, senior commissioning editor at Wiley, who understood the point of the book straight away and helped me make it even better; Elizabeth Whiley, Wiley's Professional Development editor, who worked so hard to create an outstanding final product; Chloe Peel for her social marketing skills and Maree Peel as catalyst for the publishing contract; and the hundreds of business people I talked to whose stories of awesome, interesting and absurd people practices in their organisations kept fanning the flame of my fervour.

I'd also like to thank my family and friends for their continued support; Nancy Ahern, who didn't get to read this book but would have treasured it; and of course my husband, John Ahern, who should really get joint author status on this book for the hundreds of hours he put into reading and editing drafts and for always offering outstanding advice.

INTRODUCTION

Why change?

If I were running a company today I would have one priority above all others; to acquire as many of the best people in the world.

Jim Collins, business researcher and best-selling author of *Good To Great* and *Built To Last*

According to the results of a CEO Institute survey, the number-one issue keeping chief executives awake at night is 'sourcing and retaining skilled staff'. Yet when PricewaterhouseCoopers asked 1300 global CEOs about their operational priorities[1], talent strategies didn't make the top five. So while CEOs may claim to be suffering from insomnia, it seems they're doing very little to alleviate the problem.

The question that instantly springs to mind is 'Why?' In this age when almost every company is lauding how people are their greatest asset — their number one priority, their most important resource — and with skills shortages dominating the business press, why is there so much talk and so little real action?

This question is even more perplexing when you consider the mountains of empirical evidence that demonstrate the link between attracting and keeping good people, and the business bottom line. 'Best Employer' companies achieve on average four times the profit growth of other organisations[2] and perform three times better than the general market when it comes to comparative stock market returns.[3]

Even during the global financial crisis (GFC), the US-based Parnassus Workplace Fund—a group that only invests in organisations with a solid reputation for having outstanding workplaces—had an annual average return on investment of 10.81 per cent, compared to the S&P index's 3.97 per cent. The proof really is in the profits. So when there's such an obvious prize up for grabs, the disconnect between what CEOs are thinking and saying and what they're actually doing not only doesn't make sense, it's almost self-defeating.

I became vaguely aware of this problem at the age of 25, when I got drunk at a conference and told my boss that the way the company hired and trained people was crap. (This is not a strategy that I would generally recommend!) Two weeks later he rang and asked to meet with me. I dreaded the encounter, feeling sure that he was going to sack me for my outburst. Instead, he sat me down and said if I thought I knew so much about human resources (HR), then I should turn one of the company's shops into the organisation's first recruitment and training centre. A week later I found myself standing on a street front in the middle of the city with the keys to the shop, wondering what the heck I was supposed to do. That was the start of my new vocation.

I spent the next decade and more developing and honing a system of unconventional techniques that produced extraordinary results and would eventually solve the problems of a host of organisations. I'd like to say that it came about because of Einstein-like intelligence or Branson-style business flair, but that would be fibbing. I had just three things going for me. The first was that I had no conventional training in HR: my Arts degree, majoring in journalism, was about as useful as a wet tissue when it came to HR. So I bumbled along, finding my own practical solutions to problems. I realise now how lucky that was, as I wasn't blinkered by traditional ideas.

The second advantage I had was sheer practice. The global travel company I worked for, Flight Centre Limited, was opening a new store almost every 48 hours. It was business at warp speed. As an HR leader and director, I have now interviewed more than 1000 people and because of the awful, gut-wrenching mistakes I made—particularly in the early days—and some good calls as well, I have learned a lot.

My third advantage was that, just when I thought I knew everything about recruiting and retaining people, I had the ground ripped out from under me. Shipped overseas to help start up Flight Centre in the UK, my conventional methods proved ineffective in an environment where the company was an unknown competing against well-established, 800-store travel agency chains. As if that wasn't challenge enough, as a new company director I was responsible for the growth and profits of the entire operation.

It didn't take me long to work out that good people practices would be the key to my success or demise. If I couldn't hire enough highfliers, our shops stayed empty or were so understaffed that we lost good customers. If I couldn't develop people quickly, or if they quit in the first few months, our costs blew out, morale plummeted, stress levels went up and we ended up in a cycle of destruction. These staffing factors had a far greater impact on the profitability of our small start-up enterprise than if our sales systems were a bit loose, if our books didn't quite balance, if our wholesale deals weren't too sharp or if the calls from our advertising campaigns were down. To overcome these new challenges, I was forced to attack HR from a whole new angle, and the techniques I developed eventually became the foundations of my successful 7-step system.

By the time I returned to Australia and was approached by James Carlopio, head of Bond University's Centre for Executive Education (CEE), to develop and run 'people' seminars, I had a whole batch of effective strategies. And they were now in big demand. Eighty per cent of the university's business clients—a cross-section of small to large, public and private corporations from diverse industries—had rated recruiting and retaining staff as their most urgent business issue. It was actually quite funny as I was back to where I had started: telling bosses (in a far more polite and sober way) how to improve their people processes. But this time I had a lot more answers.

'Winning the War for Talent' became the CEE's most popular workshop that year and participants across many different industries contacted me afterwards to say that they had implemented the strategies to great effect. I was over the moon to see one large, public-listed company cut staff turnover by half, improve its profits by several million dollars and resume its previously stalled global expansion plans. Others saved hundreds of thousands of dollars in direct hiring costs, filled their vacancies and were amazed at the increased happiness and productivity of their new workforce.

But what fascinated me most about this experience was that not everyone thought about people practices the way I did. Nearly everyone talked about their sourcing and retention problems as if they were reading off a menu card of external factors, such as localised skills shortages, currency changes, competing high wages or Generation Y's alleged chronic unreliability. Only the rare few thought their problems had anything to do with their own practices. And unlike other disciplines in which objective processes were the very foundation of success, good hiring—I was repeatedly told—was simply about 'gut feel', 'reading people well' or using dubious psychometric test data to justify subjective decision-making. Many stuck to this line in spite of all evidence to the contrary that existed within these businesses, such as unfilled vacancies, high staff turnover rates and, of course, disappointing profits.

So I was back to that puzzling question again. Why were organisations spraying around slogans about cherishing their employees, yet not actively doing anything of real impact to measure or improve their people practices? Why were my kind of proven techniques so rarely used in organisations, even though they produced such outstanding results? What was the real cause of this disconnect?

I stumbled onto the answer when I began looking at historical data and found that in developed countries around the world, applicants have outnumbered jobs available for nearly 100 years (as shown in figure I). Consider the economic lows culminating in the Great Depression that characterised the first half of the twentieth century when up to 20 per cent of the population was out of work; the advent of women into the workforce, which plugged the gaps in the labour market during World War II; and the population surge caused by the post-war 'baby boomers', who entered the job market in the mid 1970s and competed for vacancies for the next two decades. For nearly a century then, hiring was as easy as plucking an apple from a small tree; people were 'lucky' to have jobs, and that was how they were treated.

Figure I: the labour market in the twentieth century

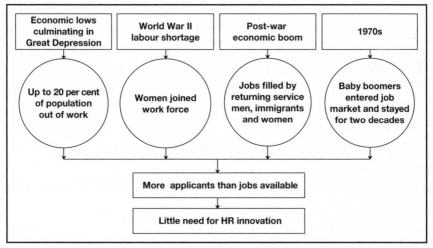

With no requirement for innovation, HR was never recognised as a key business pillar and became a backwater. This atrophy is evident by looking at conventional corporate leadership structure where there are CEOs, COOs, CFOs, CIOs, but still very few 'CROs' or 'CHROs'.

'People' people are still seldom elevated to senior levels, have little involvement in corporate discussion and strategic decision-making and are often paid less than their peers in other disciplines. It's not surprising then, that often these departments have become a dumping ground for administrative tasks such as running payroll or tracking holiday leave and workplace health and safety—jobs that have little to do with the getting and keeping of good people.

Because most companies haven't applied the same level of rigour and measurement to HR as they have to their other business systems, subjective practices have spread like a pandemic throughout the industry. The lack of accountability has also acted as a magnet for bureaucrats, so in many organisations HR has become more about control, policing and devising of ever more complex systems, rather than intelligent practices that facilitate real business outcomes. Instead of being a crucial piston in the engine of business then, the discipline has become stuck at roughly the same stage of development as professional medicine in the eighteenth century, a time when toxic mercury was used to treat many ailments and heroin was the common cure for colds.

The war for talent

This HR inertia is now unsustainable. In the late 1990s, every developed country around the world experienced high productivity and low unemployment (see figure II). Positions vacant outnumbered good applicants for the first time in nearly a century and with the power moving to the job-seeker, the 'stay for life' mentality vanished in just a few short years. Employers faced a 'war for talent' on two fronts. Not only were they competing to fill new positions, they were also fighting to keep their existing people. This double whammy meant that vacancies spiralled at the very time that many businesses were finding it almost impossible to recruit.

Figure II: the labour market 1990–2007

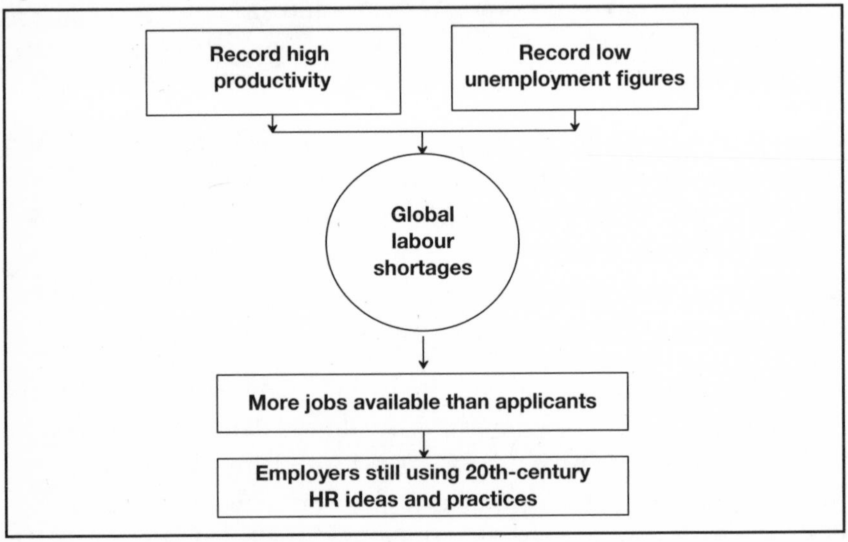

One CEO told me during this period that his staff turnover rate had soared to 60 per cent. We worked out the figures. He had 400 employees on an annual average wage of $80000, so even at the lowest estimated cost of staff turnover at 50 per cent of annual salary, this equated to $9.6 million per year.[4] He was shocked. He'd never considered staff turnover in such a tangible dollar value before so he'd never realised how much poor people practices were affecting his annual bottom line. Every 10 per cent reduction in staff turnover equated to about $1.6 million in profit increase. This became his key goal that year and while a staff turnover target of 50 per cent wasn't going to win him any awards, he'd made a significant first step.

The future

Even though the GFC that began in 2008 relieved some of this employment tension, the battle for talent is now the new reality. Companies are experiencing a paradox in that although unemployment may be high in certain countries and industries, they still struggle to attract and keep the right people. For instance, 14 million Americans were out of work in 2013, yet according to the US Bureau of Labor Statistics there were still 3.7 million unfilled jobs. These figures demonstrate the distortion of the old supply-and-demand curve. Whereas in the 'good old days' many jobs could be held by most candidates, employers now compete for a smaller pool of better-skilled recruits.

To add to the challenge, in Australia, the UK, Europe, Japan and the US the overall workforce is shrinking. As demographer Bernard Salt highlighted in his book *The Big Tilt*, baby boomers are exiting the workforce at a faster rate than the next generations are entering it.[5] Add to these factors escalating technological skills and increased competition from global employers and it is clear that the days when employing people was as easy as plucking apples are unlikely to return, as you can see in figure III (overleaf).

Figure III: the labour market from 2008 onwards

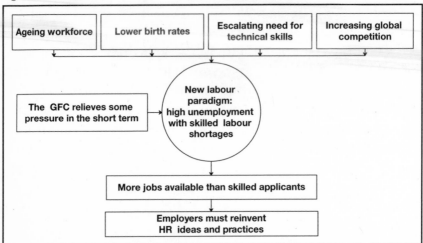

The opportunity

What people demand and expect from jobs has also changed, yet many companies haven't altered their thinking or practices. This is where there's a fantastic opportunity for employers. People rarely alter their behaviour unless forced to, so there's been little need or motivation for companies to improve or reinvent their people strategies. Yet blaming hiring failures and rising staff turnover on shifts in the labour tide, or the fact that someone offered your star recruit the latest iPhone, will no longer do. The twenty-first century is a time when continuous improvement of people processes is the new paradigm. Survival of the fittest means those who adapt and improve their current practices can snap up and retain more of the skilled and innovative candidates in the marketplace and turn the 'war for talent' to their own advantage. Those who cling to their traditional practices will struggle for growth and existence.

The Highfliers 7-step System

When I discuss the relevance of great people practices—whether it's to fill vacancies, cut employee turnover, or decrease cost and ultimately increase profit—most executives agree with me, but the difficulty lies in the method. After 100 years of HR inertia, subjective practices and stunted systems, most of them simply don't know where to start or how to do it. Conventional literature doesn't help because twentieth-century practices designed for a different labour market are useless and sometimes actively damaging to present-day business outcomes. And the shining lights of those companies that are excelling and innovating in this field are dimmed by the many traditionalists and cliché-speaking bureaucrats who have flooded the discipline. Being told to inspire, challenge, excite and have fun with your staff is all very nice but without tangible techniques it's like being given a car without the keys.

The purpose of this book is to fill this gap and arm organisations with all the tools necessary to recruit, inspire and retain great people. In the next seven chapters I will reveal my Highfliers 7-step System, a 'how to' guide of specific people practices that produce extraordinary business results. The system is illustrated in figure IV (overleaf).

Figure IV: The Highfliers 7-step System

CHAPTER 1: THE DRIVERS			What are the key drivers?
Sales	Speed	Attitude	

CHAPTER 2: THE INFRASTRUCTURE			What do we need to start?
Company attitude	HR champion	Manager involvement	
Business practices aligned with recruitment outcomes	Dedicated recruiters	Rewards and measurement	

CHAPTER 3: ATTRACTING			How do we attract the best people?
Applicant motivators	Advertising and branding	Other candidate pools	

CHAPTER 4: SCREENING			How do we screen them?
Attitude	Skills	Practical fit	

CHAPTER 5: INTERVIEWING			How do we interview them?
An exceptional first impression	Inspiring and assessing	Practical selling tools	

CHAPTER 6: ENGAGING			How do we choose and engage them?
Choosing a Highflier	An unbeatable offer	First contact	

CHAPTER 7: RETAINING			How do we retain them?
One-on-ones	Rewards and recognition	Learning and development	
Communication	Team planning	Perks	

Each step will build understanding and expertise and includes proven techniques for instant implementation. The steps are sequential, beginning with attracting and hiring the right people and moving through to effective techniques for keeping the great people who have been engaged. For the best results, I recommend reading the book one chapter at a time, analysing your business using the end-of-chapter questions and making the necessary organisational changes before moving on to the next chapter. If you do this, whether you're a three-person enterprise or a 30 000-employee corporation, I guarantee you will transform your business success.

Yet I didn't write this book just to share my effective people practices or to help CEOs sleep better at night. My goal through publication is to challenge conventional thinking as to what really drives organisational profitability and to reshape the whole conversation in this area. I want to show how the business of people management is the heart, soul and balance sheet of an organisation, move HR to the top table and make the outstanding treatment of people in the workplace the norm.

As French novelist Marcel Proust said:

> *The only real voyage of discovery consists not of seeking new landscapes but in having new eyes.*

Let's now look at the whole business of people in a different light.

Where are we now?

To begin assessing your organisation's current people practices, answer the following questions.

→ What were our recruitment achievements over the past 12 months in terms of vacancies filled, quality of novices and new systems and innovations?

→ What were our hiring disappointments over the past 12 months (that we don't want to repeat over the next 12 months)?

→ What can we learn from this?

→ What is the current staff turnover in our organisation?

→ What does this turnover cost us in terms of time and money? (Base this on 50 per cent of the average annual wage multiplied by the number who have left.)

→ What is the estimated total number of staff required over the next 12 months to achieve our business goals, using these existing turnover figures to determine estimated replacement staff and adding on new staff requirements?

→ If we were to fill all these vacant positions with suitable people, and reduce our staff turnover, what impact would this have on the organisation?

→ On a scale of 1 to 10 with 1 being the worst and 10 being the best, how would we rate recruitment in the following areas?

  o Overall effectiveness

  o Consistent systems

  o Recruiter ability

  o Objective measurement

  o Continuous improvement

→ On a scale of 1 to 10 with 1 being the worst and 10 being the best, how would our employees rate our workplace in the following areas?

  o Communication

  o Rewards and recognition

  o Learning and development

  o Work–life balance

  o Vision and leadership

→ What percentage of our employees are satisfied and fully engaged in their jobs?

CHAPTER 1

The drivers: the three secret weapons for hiring great people

When it gets too hard it usually means that you're doing something wrong.

Moira Brady, my children's first babysitter

At the lowest point of my career I discovered the three secret weapons to great hiring. They were easily implemented, didn't require unlimited funds and had been ignored by the majority of organisations. In fact, they were so rarely used that those who applied them stood out like beacons in the marketplace and achieved outstanding recruitment success.

I know this because I've been using them to great effect for more than a decade and I've filled all my vacancies, regardless of the labour market. The businesses I have applied them to have surged ahead in growth and profits, and staff turnover has been well below industry averages. Without these innovations, I would have lost my job and all future career prospects.

My transformation began when I flew into London to jointly set up Flight Centre's UK operation. With a mandate to open one shop a month, finding good employees was vital to the success of the whole operation. Having run a successful recruitment and training centre in Australia, I was confident that my HR skills were up to the challenge. Imagine my shock then, when three months later, despite receiving lots of applications, I still hadn't employed a single decent recruit.

Up to this point I'd never realised how much my company's branding had contributed to my recruitment success. In Australia, Flight Centre was a big fish with an iconic brand and a store on every street corner in every major city. As a recruiter I had my pick of hundreds of suitable candidates. In the UK we weren't even a guppy. We didn't have a single store or head office; we had no trading history, no brand recognition, no demonstrated achievements and I was interviewing people in the dining room of a rental house or at a table in the local coffee shop. My recruitment ads attracted hundreds of responses, but most of them were unsuitable.

There was only one thing to do to fix this. I panicked and increased my advertising spend in a bid to attract more good candidates. I now call this strategy 'hope recruitment'—what many companies do when they can't fill their vacancies. It operates on the conventional principle that the best way to recruit more people is to attract more people. By increasing the size, number and colour of recruitment ads, upping salary offers and even throwing in extravagant extras such as gym memberships, car leasing or iPhones to sweeten the deal, organisations hope to improve their recruitment success.

I realised what a poor strategy this was when I still failed to fill my vacancies. As figure 1.1 shows, in a market with a diminishing pool of suitable applicants, organisations that practise 'hope recruitment' engage in a never-ending cycle of spending more and more dollars for less and less return. Even though money is not the answer, many businesses continue down this path because they have no other mechanism for dealing with recruitment failure.

Figure 1.1: the 'hope recruitment' cycle

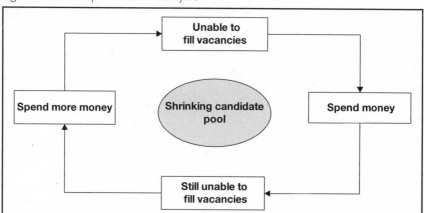

This was the dilemma I found myself in. I could see that spending money wasn't working, but I just couldn't see any other way forward. My recruitment problems reverberated like a constant echo in my head: 'Who wants to work for a company that they've never even heard of? It's impossible to get good staff. Our tiny start-up company can't compete with the industry megabrands. Maybe our wages aren't high enough. No-one will take a job when they're interviewed at someone's dining room table'.

Then it hit me one morning that I was doing something that had always annoyed me in others: I was externalising.

As a leader, I'd spent half of my work life coaching people to confront and deal with challenges head on, yet here I was, just as guilty, making up excuses for my poor results. I thought long and hard about this and began to comprehend that perhaps this was the true cause of my dilemma. As my children's babysitter used to say, when things get too hard, it's often because you are doing something wrong. Maybe the way I was thinking about the problem *was* the problem. Maybe I needed to look at it with new eyes.

I thought back to the employees I'd dealt with in the past who had also blamed their poor results on external factors. This was common in underperforming salespeople: their store was located in the wrong place, there weren't enough people walking past or head office was filled with a bunch of bureaucrats who didn't understand the retail business and weren't running enough ads. Yet as area leader, when I asked them to write down their sales enquiries for a week and draw a line through the ones that had actually resulted in a booking, I discovered they were only converting a small proportion of their customers, as per the example in figure 1.2. The truth was that they didn't need more clients. They just needed to hone their sales skills and systems to convert more of the enquiries they already had.

Figure 1.2: customer conversion rate

Enquiries per week:	100
Bookings:	20
Conversion rate:	Bookings (20) ÷ enquiries (100) = 0.2
	$0.2 \times 100 = 20$ per cent of customers
Therefore 80 per cent of customers weren't booking.	

Thinking about the example in figure 1.2, I decided to apply this same lesson to recruitment. It was my attitude that was the problem. Because of Flight Centre's sexy brand image in Australia, I'd never had to develop any skill in converting applicants into employees. Like poor salespeople who focus on quoting, not closing, I was just an interviewer sifting away, not a dedicated recruiter. Yet closing was crucial to my success in the UK. I didn't need to attract hundreds of suitable applicants. I already had a few decent CVs. I just needed to hone my recruitment processes so that I hired *all* the good candidates who were already applying. In essence:

> effective attraction + effective recruitment processes
> = hiring success

I didn't realise it at the time, but this was a major turning point in my recruitment career.

I invented a new term based on the sales discipline—the recruitment conversion rate (RCR)—to measure the percentage of *suitable* candidates who applied for the job and ended up being employed. It works like this: take the number of suitable applicants employed, divide this by the number of suitable CVs received and multiply the result by 100. When I did the maths on the effect of improving the conversion rate, I began to get really excited.

As figure 1.3 shows, during my 'good old days' in Australia, where my organisation's branding attracted a lot of suitable candidates, I could recruit enough good people without even really trying. In the UK, I was only receiving an average of four suitable applications per position advertised out of the many who applied, however, I had to become so good at recruitment—and make my hiring process so applicant friendly, engaging and stimulating—that every one of those four would want to come and work for my organisation.

Figure 1.3: effect of improving the recruitment conversion rate (RCR)

Goal: 3 new people

The 'good old picking apples' days:

Total applicants attracted from advertising	100
Suitable applicants (say 20 per cent)	20
Average recruitment conversion rate	**30 per cent**
Suitable applicants employed	3 (with 3 others knocked back)

In a tough labour market:

Total applicants attracted from advertising	20
Suitable applicants (say 20 per cent)	4
Average recruitment conversion rate	**30 per cent**
Suitable applicants employed	1 (plus 2 more from the 'unsuitable candidate' pool)

After improving the conversion rate:

Total applicants attracted from advertising	20
Suitable applicants (say 20 per cent)	4
Average recruitment conversion rate	**75 per cent**
Suitable applicants employed	3

My new recruitment mantra became:

Focus on converting the suitable applicants, not just on increasing the total number of applicants.

Once an organisation embraces this, it has started on a new winning path because most of its competitors won't comprehend or assess the effect their hiring practices have on suitable applicants.

I now needed some measuring systems, but I couldn't source anyone who was applying objective KPIs to recruitment. In the end I invented some tools so I could assess and track the improvement in my recruitment conversion rate percentage. From then on, when anyone said to me, 'The employment market is tough', or 'It's impossible to find good staff', I would ask them the following questions:

- How many suitable people are applying?

- How many are dropping out before or after your interviews?

- What is your current recruitment conversion rate?

- What are you doing to improve your recruitment processes to increase this rate?

- What impact does reducing your failure rate have on company profits?

I love asking the profit question because it focuses people on outcomes, not bureaucratic processes. So often HR departments operate in a vacuum, disconnected from the bottom line. The reality is that they should be the profit-driving champions of every organisation.

The three secret weapons to great recruitment

Once I'd grasped the essential importance of focusing on suitable applicants, I had to come up with some innovations to get these few great people every time. This wasn't easy. It was uncharted territory and there weren't any reference books with practical solutions that could help me. Most were filled with theory, jargon and clichés. I was forced to fall back on my own resources and experiment to find answers. In time I came up with the three secret weapons that would drive my recruitment success and become powerhouse tools for any company that used them in their own war for talent.

Secret weapon number 1

The first powerhouse strategy occurred to me when I was out having a coffee with a UK colleague one morning.

'You know, competing for good employees here is as difficult as competing for customers,' I grumbled. Then I stopped and thought about what I'd just said.

'Gotta go.' I jumped up and ran back to my desk.

I had had a flashback to when I first started selling travel. I was an average salesperson and couldn't figure out why I wasn't making much money. Then one day Robyn, a temp, came to work in the office and booked 12 of her 15 enquiries. Listening to her talk, I realised that the difference between Robyn and me was that she paid attention to each customer and focused on understanding their needs to get the booking. I, on the other hand, was concentrating on the mechanical process of the enquiry, rushing through each interaction so I could serve the next person waiting in line at the counter. This was the conversion rate analogy in action and was a revelation to me. I changed my strategy and that year I won one of the company's 'Million Dollar Consultant' awards for outstanding sales.

Pondering this episode I realised that I needed to think of recruitment in these terms. As Stephen Covey, best-selling author of *The 7 Habits of Highly Effective People,* wrote: 'First seek to understand … then to be understood'. Like any traditional recruiter, I'd been focusing my time and energy on what I wanted from applicants and I hadn't expended much real effort on considering what the candidates actually might want: what would make them more likely to sign up with me.

If I was going to convert great people into employees, then I needed to invert my thinking. I needed to break away from the accepted paradigm that they would be lucky to be employed—to flip it around and recognise that I was fortunate if they chose to work for me. *I needed to convince good people that my role and my organisation was the right fit for them.* This was Sales 101 at its most basic and it became my first secret ingredient of recruitment.

> ➤ **Secret weapon number 1: Recruitment is a sales process.**

I started experimenting and drew on sales strategies that I could apply to every stage of recruitment—from creating a great first impression, to selling the benefits, to closing the sale so that suitable applicants always signed up with me—and an after-sales service system to make sure I retained every one of my new recruits.

I'll outline the sales techniques that can be applied step by step in this book. What's important from this point on is to think of recruitment as a front-line sales process. You, the employer, must do everything possible to get the right person—not put the onus on them to fill your vacancies. You're lucky to have a person willing to invest their time and skill in your company—not the other way around. Chapter 3 in particular shows how an organisation can put this principle into active practice to achieve outstanding success.

Secret weapon number 2

While experimenting with sales techniques I stumbled across the second key business driver in my recruitment revolution. It was simple to apply, cost no money and is underestimated and underused by almost every organisation I've ever dealt with.

I discovered it when I began to analyse why I hadn't hired any of the suitable candidates who had sent me their CVs. I'd developed the pitch and an effective package, but I was still failing. Thinking about it from their point of view, one factor became very clear. People don't like being out of work, or in limbo, for very long and good applicants never will be. It had taken me three weeks from the time I'd received their CVs to the day I called them in for an interview and in the interim many had accepted other job offers. It was obvious that if I was going to employ the best recruits, I had to recruit faster than any of my competitors. Like Tom Cruise in the movie *Top Gun*, suddenly I felt the need for speed.

The following week I started experimenting again. I placed an ad, read every CV the day it arrived and rang the suitable candidates straight away to book an interview. If they were good, I offered them a job within 24 hours. I worried that this might reek of desperation, but on the contrary, people took it as a positive and I had my pick of the best applicants. Even better, within two weeks I had recruited six people—six *good* people!

One of the six was an employee called Chris, who went on to become one of the company's managing directors several years later. At a conference a few months after I hired him I asked him why he'd taken the job.

He looked at me and grinned. 'Mandy,' he said, 'I had been to lots of interviews before you rang but you made the first job offer. I figured a bird in the hand was worth two in the bush'.

I thought about this. 'Hang on,' I queried, 'you said I made the first job offer. Does that mean you had others?'

He laughed. 'I was offered another three the following week. But I'd already taken yours and I didn't want to go back on my word.'

We both took a sip of wine and then I decided to go in for the kill. 'So—scruples question—if you had been offered all four jobs at the same time, which one would you have taken?'

He grinned sheepishly before replying. 'Not yours.'

I laughed out loud. And so this became my second secret weapon.

> ➤ **Secret weapon number 2: Speed!**

From then on speed became a lethal warhead in my recruitment process and my success rate soared. Figure 1.4 (overleaf) shows how this works by comparing two companies competing for the same new recruits. Company B, which is using speed as a conscious tool, offers suitable candidates a position before other companies have even interviewed them, so it gets all the good recruits. By the time Company A interviews the applicants, only the unsuitable ones are left. It then has to choose the best of these, which means it employs poor recruits and guarantees itself one of two things: high future staff turnover and/or poorer individual results, beginning a cycle of self-destruction.

Figure 1.4: the effect of speed in recruiting suitable applicants

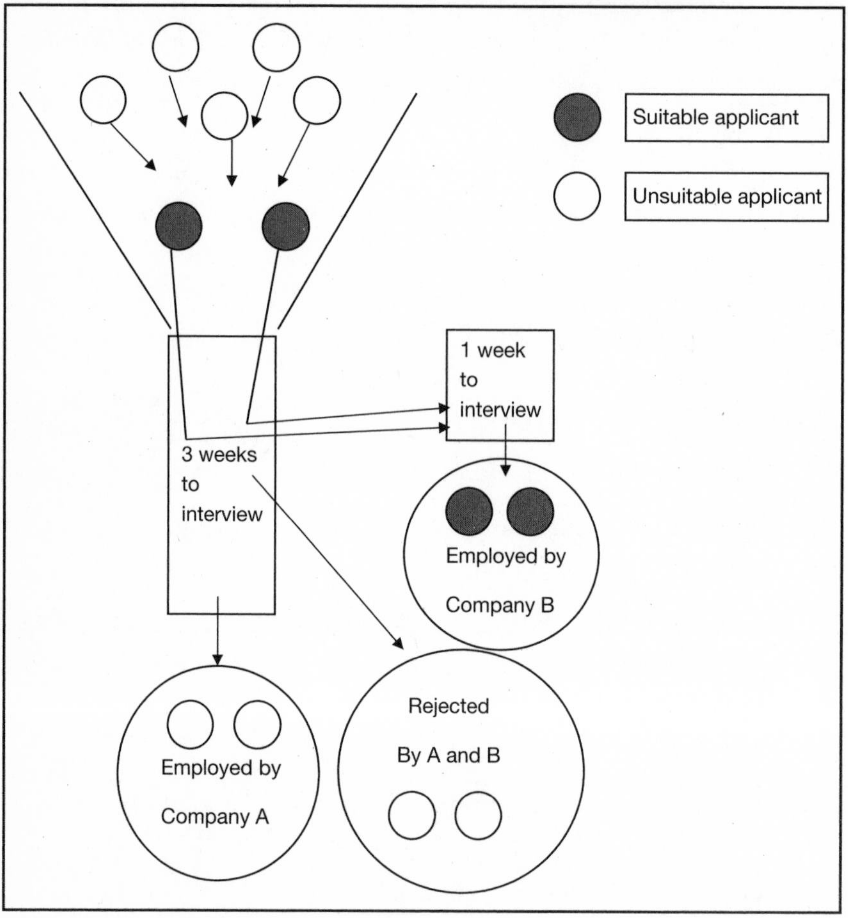

This is one of the most important lessons I learned about recruitment. When organisations say there are no suitable candidates, it's often because they've moved too slowly in the recruitment process, just as I'd done. They've taken too long to read CVs and the applicants have dropped out before they've even contacted them. Or the organisation's interview process is so long and arduous that many suitable applicants have given up in disgust. Or the potential candidate has received another offer while the recruiter is running endless psychometric tests and background checks.

Ironically, the reason executives often want to slow down the hiring process is because of their poor recruitment systems. They say, 'We need to take our time to make sure we get the right person', and quote the adage, 'hire slow, fire fast', but this is because they have no tools to apply to determine the right person in any objective manner in the first place.

Where the organisation does need to slow down is in the *pre-recruiting stage*. They need to develop well-thought-out, rigorous processes such as an attractive ad template, effective screening and selling tools, and an inspiring interview process. Putting some thought into these kinds of practices is the fundamental meaning of 'hire slow' and enables recruiters to act with decisive speed in the period from advertising to job offer, where swiftness is vital to the outcome.

The principles of applying speed to recruitment

There are some basic principles underlying the secret weapon of speed in regards to recruitment.

- *The most suitable applicants apply within the first five days of advertising.* I placed a recruitment ad every Saturday and tracked the results for a year. Ninety per cent of my best recruits had applied within five days of advertising. Motivated achievers wanted to do something straight away. It's not a blanket rule as the other 10 per cent accounts for the fact that someone may be on holidays or may have missed the original ad.

- *Interviewing applicants quickly gives them a positive, dynamic first impression of the company.* They also take it as a compliment that the organisation has recognised their worth by moving so fast.

- *Good candidates are more likely to take a job offer that already exists.* They prefer to do this than to wait for the outcome of further interviews.

- *By offering a good candidate a position before other companies have even interviewed, an organisation can avoid bidding wars.* The issue of competing salaries rarely comes up.

- *Making a person a job offer the day after their interview doubles the likelihood of acceptance.* When I first started speeding up my recruitment process, I made the mistake of offering people the job on the same day as their interview and I suffered many knockbacks. This strategy made the organisation appear desperate, so the candidates were less likely to take the position. My success rate doubled when I made the offer the following day and came up with an offer process that was tailored to the person, showing that we really did feel fortunate to employ them.

I've since read of other companies that have used the speed principle with outstanding success. The Ritz-Carlton hotel group, two times winner of America's prestigious Malcolm Baldridge National Quality Award, reduced the time taken to process new hires from application to job offer from 21 days to less than a week. Their staff turnover dropped from a high of 77 per cent to just under 30 per cent, well below the industry standard. As they noted in their Baldridge application, 'We have no competitive comparisons … we know of no other company that does the hiring process quicker'.

I explained the speed principle to a client of mine who was having problems filling vacancies. One of his store managers had been doing all of his hiring in her spare time, so after talking to me, he took her out of her existing shop and made her a full-time recruiter. The results astounded him. Even though her recruitment system hadn't changed and wasn't even that good, she now applied it at much greater speed, and not only did they fill all their vacancies, but they recruited much better candidates as well.

The rule also applies in reverse. A few years ago the Australian Defence Force (ADF) initiated a multi million-dollar recruitment drive as it was struggling to fill vacancies. The organisation announced that it was spending $30 million on the advertising alone. This sounded like hope recruitment to me.

A few months later I read that the Defence Minister, after a number of complaints, had announced a free hotline number that applicants could call to check on the progress of their application as he'd discovered that on average, the recruitment process was taking 31 weeks.[6] I was horrified. Thirty-one weeks! In my view, the best applicants would have been snapped up by other employers long before this, negating the time, money and effort put into attracting them in the first place. I wasn't surprised to read more media articles about the ADF's ongoing staffing issues in the months after this campaign.

Corporate culture is often the biggest handicap when it comes to applying speed to recruitment. An HR leader for a large mining company complained to me that it took her eight weeks to recruit because of all the background checks that were required. It was a no-win situation for her. If she didn't conduct the checks she was at fault, and then she was also in trouble for not filling positions, because the length of time taken for the background checks meant she lost all the good recruits.

In order to increase her success she had to first educate company executives in the reality that every day added onto the recruitment process reduced the number of vacancies filled. She wasn't able to change these long-established procedures, however, and she still employs the leftovers. The company struggles on with a very high staff turnover, unaware of the money it could be making if it employed more suitable candidates.

Secret weapon number 3

Sales and speed will make some incredible inroads, but they're blunt tools without the third secret weapon, which is the keystone to a successful recruitment system. This factor is one that I've always been aware of, but it wasn't until I experienced hiring difficulties in the UK that I began to apply it as a conscious tool. By creating systems and processes around its use, I turned it into a powerful recruitment mechanism that became the final pillar for all my future achievements.

The breakthrough came after I'd applied speed and sales to my recruitment process and still couldn't fill all my vacancies. Now that I knew it was just a question of the way I saw the problem, I decided to put every step of my hiring process under the microscope. It didn't take me long to work out that the final snag lay in the way I was personally identifying and screening people.

It's standard practice for most organisations to base their candidate identification and screening around work skills. Open up any newspaper and the career ads focus on such criteria as an accounting degree, a high school certificate, three years' experience in sales or maybe a forklift licence. Because skills are easy to quantify—an applicant either has them or they don't—the recruiter only has to tick a box to decide whether to proceed with an interview.

I discovered that using work skills to identify recruits didn't take into account other important aspects of the person. This becomes obvious when you think about why people don't succeed in roles. They may fight with their co-workers; be late for work; never finish projects on time; be unprofessional in meetings; have affairs with subordinates; or even steal money. None of these factors has anything to do with their skills or qualifications as you can see in figure 1.5.

Figure 1.5: a common recruitment cycle when applicants are identified by skill alone

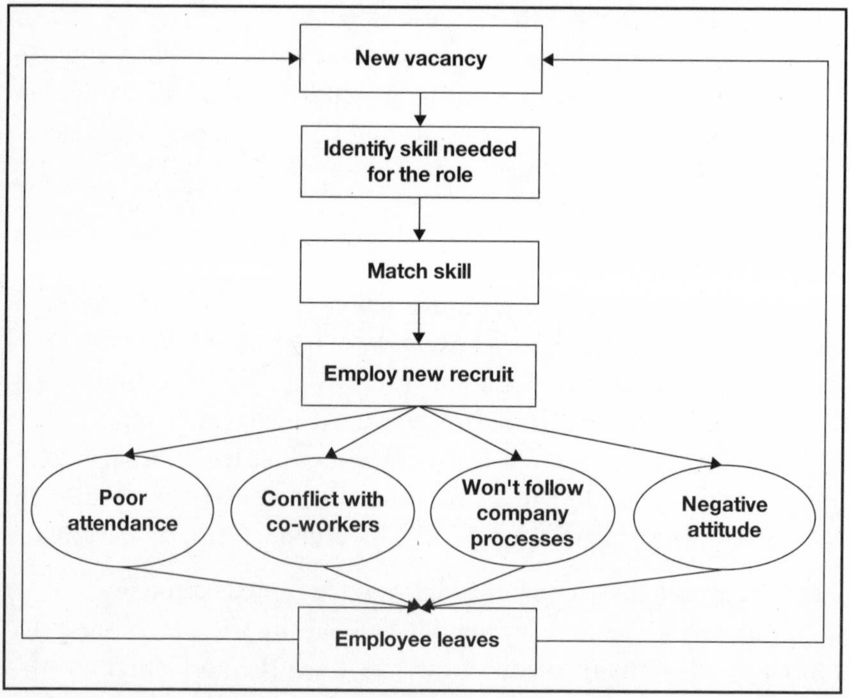

It also knocks out many great recruits. Two of the most successful travel consultants I worked with were previously a butcher and

a tennis coach respectively, with no prior sales experience. If these people had been identified solely on technical skills they wouldn't have landed their jobs in the first place. The same applies to many prominent corporate achievers. Bill Gates of Microsoft fame and Mark Zuckerberg, founder of Facebook, both dropped out of Harvard; Richard Branson, CEO of the Virgin group, left school at 16. It's ironic that these talented people would be rejected by most modern-day companies—possibly even including their own companies—because of their lack of qualifications.

Skill, then, is only part of the screening equation. Over time I worked out that there was another factor at work, one that had a much greater bearing on recruiting great people. It was difficult to measure and it would take time and effort to build it into an effective screening system (which I discuss in chapter 4). When I applied it, however, not only did I fill all my vacancies, I also reduced my staff turnover rates. I've since used it in a number of businesses, both public and private, all with the same positive result.

The crucial factor I identified was *attitude*.

> ➤ **Secret weapon number 3: Recruit for attitude, train for skill!**

A person's attitudes are key to their future achievement. If someone's outlook is negative, this will colour all their relationships and dealings. There's no magic 'off' switch when they enter the corporate world. The opposite also applies. Positive, committed people apply themselves with gusto to every endeavour. Common sense, then, says that applicants with good attitudes make the best employees.

Once I recognised how critical this was, the first step was to identify which attitudes were essential for achievement and how I could turn this into a tangible system. But to do that was a bit like catching butterflies without a net. During an interview, all candidates tell you how positive, keen and dynamic they are, but I needed to determine this in reality. There was little about practical application written on this subject so again I began experimenting. I analysed the results of hundreds of interviews and worked out the attitudes that were shared by my most successful recruits.

The top 5 attitudes of successful recruits

Here's my list of top 5 attitudes for great recruits in any job role.

1 *Positive work ethic.* No matter what technical skills a person may demonstrate, if they don't have a positive approach to working, they will never be successful. Those who enjoy applying themselves and reaping a reward for their work make the best recruits.

2 *Perseverance.* I learned a valuable lesson about perseverance when writing my first book, *Family Village Tribe.* As part of my research I interviewed the top 50 salespeople, out of more than 5000, for a large global company. I was amazed to discover that most of them didn't have what I would have considered conventional attributes for sales success. Few of them had any previous sales experience and they weren't endowed with scintillating social skills or oozing with charisma. The only factor they had in common was an overwhelming determination to succeed.

   As time goes by, I find more and more evidence that this is almost all one needs to make great achievements in life. It's perhaps the most crucial element in recruitment as it is a prime indicator for retention. When faced with challenges and difficulties, candidates with perseverance will stay and look for solutions; those without it will move on to another company.

3 *Achievement.* Good work ethics and perseverance are important, but many roles also require candidates to continue growing and developing. If this is the case, then a background of demonstrated achievement is important. Otherwise an organisation may find itself with a recruit who has a disastrous combination of ineffectiveness and perseverance. The result: they are useless and they stay forever.

4 *Ability to work with people without continuous conflict.* A candidate's ability to get along with co-workers is key to their retention.

5 *Commitment to the job role/company.* A candidate may be a brilliant, skilled applicant, but without any demonstrated commitment to the job or the organisation they will either drop out during the recruitment process or turn over as soon as another exciting job appears on their radar. The recruiter will find themselves doing a lot of interviewing, the trainer a lot of training and the company a lot of spending if they don't weed out these applicants.

Once I'd identified the key attitudes for recruitment success, I began to see a whole new way forward for my recruitment process. I realised that if attitude *was* the key to corporate achievement then in a tight labour market I should be able to recruit people with the five desired attitudes and then train them in the core work skills. Rather than competing with my rivals for technically skilled recruits, I could source suitable candidates with good attitudes from varied backgrounds to meet all my business needs. I'd have to exclude highly specialised roles, but this approach was viable for a host of corporate vacancies.

To fill the travel positions, I began to advertise for people with demonstrated achievement in any field and the response exceeded all my expectations. Matthew, an archaeologist, was a typical applicant. Tired of working overseas in remote locations, he was searching for a challenging career change that didn't involve years of retraining. He was intelligent, articulate and passionate about travel and learned the sales and technical information required to be a travel consultant in record time. Together with an ex–postal manager, a schoolteacher and a car salesman, he started a new store in Bromley, an outer suburb of London, and this became a profitable operation within 12 months.

Because these new recruits brought a wide range of life experiences to the job, the clients loved them and this became a real point of difference, compared to many competitors who often employed 17-year-old school leavers. Even better, because the new people were highly motivated and had great attitudes, within two years all four became team leaders of new stores as well. The measure also brought some external accolades. In 2003, Flight Centre's small UK operation placed first in the leadership category and third in the overall category of *The Sunday Times*'s Employer of the Year awards, surprising the retail industry and beating much larger and longer established competitors such as Marks & Spencer and Tesco.

I've now recruited for attitude in many businesses and industries with great success. This practice has helped others as well. A small commercial real estate company with 10 employees had been struggling for years because it couldn't compete with the bigger organisations when it came to recruiting good real estate salespeople. After the owner read about the concept of recruiting for attitude in my first book, he decided to advertise for sales achievers from *any* industry and train them up into real estate. He filled all his vacancies with people who'd had great success selling wine, printer cartridges and photocopiers. Within 12 months the organisation's net profit was 50 per cent higher than any year on record.

Organisations often balk at recruiting for attitude because they don't want to take the time to train people in the skills required. Yet high-achieving, persevering individuals learn fast and, unlike experienced recruits, they don't have ingrained habits or expectations that may be inhibitors in the new role.

The time taken to train a motivated but unskilled recruit is always less than that spent performance managing the poor practices and ingrained bad habits of the experienced candidate with a poor attitude. Even better, the recruit with a good attitude almost always achieves corporate results that exceed expectations.

Over time I discovered that my new attitude-focused strategy brought some other unforeseen benefits as well. For a start, it increased innovation, workforce diversity and was much more egalitarian. The successful candidate could be any age, gender or race. They may be the 57-year-old bookkeeper with the positive approach to work rather than the 25-year-old chartered accountant with a rude, aggressive manner. Or they may be the 19-year-old, ambitious, hard worker rather than the jaded 45-year-old looking for an easy ride. These people recognise when they're being given a real 'out-of-the-box' opportunity so they have more vested loyalty too.

Adding attitude as a screening factor saved a lot of time as well. There may be 50 candidates with the required technical skills, but only five with the right attitude, so by screening for this at CV stage a lot less interviewing was required. Candidates also found it easier to accept their unsuitability for a position. Because my interview questions were built around attitude, the applicant got a clear understanding of the qualities required to be successful in the role and in the organisation. Many of those who were a poor fit identified this themselves during the screening process and chose to drop out.

Recruiting people for attitude seems like common sense to me now, yet it's still quite rare in practice. Many organisations still recruit people based on their skills and then try to train for attitude. Front-line managers are often the worst offenders because they want to do as little skills training as possible to minimise time away from their income-producing roles and then they discover that dealing with the bad attitude of the person they've employed is taking up hours of their time in performance management.

Applying speed, sales and attitude to the recruitment process

With knowledge of the combined power of sales, speed and attitude, a business can begin reworking its recruitment processes. This is what I did. I built a new system from the ground up, trialling and testing strategies, and developing tools and processes that increased my hiring and retention success.

In the end, what had been my biggest problem—how to recruit in a tight labour market—gave my HR career its greatest boost. When the war for talent began, the solutions I'd been forced to come up with were so effective that I was able to apply them with great results to other organisations as well. In effect, I broke away from conventional systems and became a student of change. When it comes to twenty-first-century people practices, this may be the only constant.

The three secret weapons

To assess how well your organisation applies the three key drivers, answer the following questions.

→ How many suitable people are applying for our jobs, then dropping out before or after an interview? Are we measuring this objectively?

→ What is our current average recruitment conversion rate—that is, the number of suitable applicants employed, divided by the number of suitable CVs received, multiplied by 100?

→ How would we rate our recruitment as a sales process on a scale of 1 to 10, with 1 being the worst and 10 being the best?

→ What can we do to make our hiring process more attractive to candidates?

→ How long, in days, does it take us to recruit, from when we receive a CV to when we make an offer?

→ To improve our hiring success, how can we reduce this time frame?

→ Do we recruit for skills or attitude?

→ What effect would recruiting people for attitude have on our organisation?

CHAPTER 2

The infrastructure: the six bones of great recruitment

Believe you are defeated, believe it long enough, and it is likely to become a fact.

Norman Vincent Peale, author of
The Power of Positive Thinking

In the same way as an accounting department needs good auditors and an efficient financial operating system, or an IT division needs up-to-date software and technical experts, a recruitment practice needs the right structure in place—a robust skeleton—to be successful. This is what I call 'the six bones of great recruitment'.

I'd never realised how important these 'bones' were until the first time I worked in a company that didn't have any of this core structure in place. This was an experience I had prior to setting up my own consultancy business and it came about because I was worried that my HR system might be too 'travel industry centric'. Concerned that my techniques might not work in other organisations, I realised there was only one way to find out: I had to go undercover.

Going undercover

So, despite the protestations of my husband (who thought I was mad), I signed on with a temp agency and was eventually offered a four-week placement as an HR administration officer, at $22 per hour, in a business that built yachts. This was the perfect role for me. I knew nothing about boats and had never recruited any type of tradespeople before.

On my first day I was directed to the recruitment office—a small, dingy, windowless room located directly off the factory floor. There I met the HR manager, Teresa, who pointed me to a desk with a mountain of papers on it.

'Those on the left-hand side are staff records that I need you to file.'

'What about those ones?' I pointed at the pile on the right, which was twice as high.

She explained that they were the CVs from the past three months. 'I haven't had a chance to look at them yet, so I thought I'd get you to go through them and pull out anyone who looks promising.'

'Wow,' I said, 'that's a lot of CVs'.

'Yep, that's because we need a lot of people. We've got 88 vacancies at the moment.'

I thought she had a stutter. 'Did you say eight?' I asked.

'No,' she sighed, 'eighty-eight'.

She then pointed to a whiteboard that was covered in position names.

'We've got such demand for our yachts that we can't keep up. We had to knock back a huge order last week because we couldn't deliver. It's simply impossible to find good people at the moment.'

This sounded horrific to me. The job market was obviously far worse than I'd imagined. When I asked her how many vacancies she was filling each month she replied, 'About three'.

My mind reeled. At that rate it would take two and a half years just to fill the existing vacancies.

I asked which tools the organisation used for hiring. There weren't any. No documents for selling the benefits of the company; no well-crafted welcome letters to create a good first impression; no standard contracts; and no kits with useful information for when new employees started. This was going to make my job difficult.

The organisation did have an impressive job ad, however. It was a full-page colour spread with a yacht ploughing through crystalline blue waters. Teresa told me they ran the ad in the state and national papers and on job search websites every weekend, at $20 000 a pop. This added up to a whopping one million dollars a year. These guys were really desperate for staff. She then asked me to recruit five junior positions but wanted me to do the filing first. That took me two days.

In the meantime, the two other HR people worked on payroll administration, performance reviews, disciplinary procedures, and health and safety inductions. It was as though they'd swallowed an HR thesaurus. No-one did anything related to recruitment.

I wondered what the CEO thought about all this, but when I asked Teresa I was told he was based in the US and never showed much interest in HR on his infrequent visits. It was actually Susan, the Chief Financial Officer (CFO) who oversaw the department, which put me on instant alert as I've found almost without fail that when HR reports to a CFO, the area becomes all about administration and not so much about people. I soon found out that the CFO had no hiring knowledge or expertise, was a micro-manager, treated the HR staff as her own personal secretarial service and overruled many of their informed decisions. This didn't bode well for innovation.

When I was introduced to Susan at the end of day two, I made a subtle attempt at suggesting that perhaps if someone in the HR department actually worked on recruitment, then the company might fill more of its vacancies. She just repeated the mantra I'd already heard from HR: 'We're doing everything we can, but the employment market is tough. There are no suitable candidates out there. The mining companies are taking all the good people and pushing up the salaries so we can't match them. Generation Y are a lazy bunch—they don't want to work. We're in a niche market so it's impossible to find the specialised people we need'.

On it went. Recruitment was hard, really hard. Yes, I knew that, but flushing one million dollars a year down the toilet and losing massive contracts seemed much harder to me.

Later on I started talking to some of the supervisors in the lunch room to get a better understanding of the organisation and the job roles. I was treated with caution, almost suspicion. No-one from HR or management had ever shown this kind of interest before, but as I was just a junior temp they finally opened up to me. The conversations were revealing. Everyone I talked to was stressed as a result of the chronic understaffing. Many were working excessive hours of overtime, often coming back in on their days off to meet deadlines, and the constant flare-ups were adding to the staff turnover. The impression they gave me was that the company was ready to melt down.

Bone 1: a positive and proactive corporate attitude towards recruitment

I went home that night and thought about the organisation. Here was a profitable business with a fantastic brand and triple-A clients. It was staffed by passionate, hard-working people and its product was of the very highest quality. At the same time it was imploding as more and more good staff left through overwork because of the many unfilled vacancies. And yet, no-one was doing anything about it.

There was a raging disconnection between recruitment and its effect on the business growth and profits. The leaders obviously weren't dumb. They'd built a good company from scratch. But recruitment wasn't seen as a vital piston in the company's engine room. This corporate attitude meant that rather than attacking hiring difficulties head-on, the company simply externalised the problem and tried to compensate for it via expensive advertising. They couldn't see that it was their own beliefs that were crushing them.

I couldn't imagine this happening in other disciplines. If sales were down by 75 per cent, or the accounts showed a discrepancy of several hundred thousand dollars, I was sure the organisation's response would be very different. For genuine recruitment reform to take place, executives needed to stop believing that they were defeated before they even began. This was the only way the company was ever going to fill its vacancies.

Bone 2: an HR champion with direct access to the company leader

This negative corporate attitude towards recruitment also had a direct impact on the make-up of the HR department. It was really just an administration area and Teresa operated more like the head of a secretarial service than an HR leader. She had no mandate to be an HR champion, someone who was positive about hiring and 100 per cent focused on getting and keeping good staff, and this stymied any real hiring reform.

Yet just having a champion isn't enough if that champion doesn't have access to the business leader to explain how hiring outcomes affect profit goals. They need to have real influence at the top table and get approval for the changes required to keep improving this area. In Teresa's case, without input, engagement and buy-in from the CEO, the modifications required at many levels of the business to facilitate recruitment success were never going to happen.

Going rogue

As no-one in the yachting company showed any interest in being an HR champion, I decided it had better be me. So I went rogue. The next day I stuffed the stack of employee files into a drawer and began wading through the pile of CVs on my desk. Of the 300 resumes, nearly 200 were more than eight weeks old. 'Not good,' I thought. I identified 12 excellent potential candidates and snuck into an empty room to call them. By midday I was beaten. Every single one had already taken another position. I reverted to my 'B' list—another 15 candidates. Thirteen of the 15 had also taken other jobs. The words 'speed, speed, speed' hurtled through my brain.

I organised to interview one of the two B-graders the next day. Now all I had to arrange was somewhere to meet them. As the HR office was generally in use, I discovered that interviews were conducted on an old couch outside the door, with the deafening noise of the machine tools drowning out most of the conversation. This definitely failed my 'make a great first impression' test. Despite the poor surrounds, the applicant accepted my offer. Phew! One person employed. Eighty-seven to go.

The following week, after the 20 000-dollar cannon boomed again, firing ads in all directions, I read every résumé as it arrived, rang the good applicants and arranged interviews. I also did a hush–hush deal with the office receptionist to use a Sydney-based executive's office as my interview room. It had a model of a yacht on the desk, teak display cabinets and picturesque views from its window. It was a big step up from the couch.

From here on, it was smoother sailing. I knew little about boat building or cabinet making but I organised for the line managers to join me and I handed the interview over to them halfway through to ask the technical skills questions. By the end of the second week I'd employed five good people.

Bone 3: involvement of line managers in the recruitment process

Inadvertently, I'd also broken the rules again. I discovered that the company didn't normally include line managers in the recruitment process. Hiring was considered the sole responsibility of the HR department, even though their inadequate understanding of the technical skills required meant that the managers were often lumped with poor recruits, with little recourse. To make matters worse, these bad decisions were enforced in a militant fashion, so the end result was major hostility towards all things HR throughout the company and a high turnover of new staff.

I've always included line managers in some shape or form in the hiring process because an important factor in retaining an employee is their relationship with their immediate supervisor. I can recruit the best applicant in the country but once they start in the role it's their relationship with their manager that will primarily determine whether they stay or leave. If this leader takes ownership of the new recruit it increases the statistical chances of retention.

The manager's involvement can take many forms. My standard practice is that the recruiter handles prospective applicants from start to finish — screening them for the position and making objective recommendations — and then includes the manager when deciding on selection criteria and/or in the interview or decision-making process. Often their participation may be just a single phone conversation to discuss the attributes of the final shortlisted candidates. This does, however, give the manager a realistic idea of the calibre of recruits in the marketplace.

Involving the manager in some form also increases their recruitment proficiency and understanding. Once they see the time, effort and skill required to find the right person for a role, they're less likely to treat their new recruit as a disposable commodity.

Off the leash

When I came back at the start of the third week, I was shocked to hear Teresa had employed another temp to do the filing. I suspected the CFO had sniffed out my unauthorised activities until Teresa smiled and handed me the remaining 82 vacancy folders.

'We want you just to focus on recruitment,' she said. 'Go for it! Don't do anything else!'

I was finally off the leash. Even the CFO endorsed this activity. After all, she was now able to report some positive staffing news to the CEO. I systematically worked my way through all the current CVs, conducted 24 interviews and employed another 11 good people that week.

By now I was having fun. It was the lowest paid job I had had in years but it was such a meaty challenge.

Bone 4: the alignment of business practices with good recruitment outcomes

There were still many more hurdles to come. I discovered the company had lots of rules and regulations that were counterproductive to filling vacancies. One department was desperate for a metal polisher, but when I found a Picasso of metal polishing, who was ready to start straight away, I was told that inductions only occurred every second Monday. The guy couldn't wait around as it would have meant two weeks without pay and the executives simply couldn't see it from the candidate's point of view. I had to fight for common sense to prevail and get a special one-off induction approved.

Similarly, when it came to wages, the organisation lacked any kind of flexibility. Everyone was paid a set salary and a lack of incentives or bonuses meant there was no room for movement via negotiation. For instance, boat builders were scarce but after two weeks of searching I finally found one available whose existing wage was $300 per year more than the sum on offer. The company refused to match his salary, even though they'd just paid out another $20000 in recruitment advertising that week to get him in the door and the yacht they were working on was six weeks behind schedule with late penalties that ran into tens of thousands of dollars.

This seemed insane to me and highlighted why it's impossible to achieve success in recruitment without the ongoing modification of business practices. These have a huge impact on prospective candidates and are often the deciding factor in hiring success. Modifying shift times to make them more family friendly or changing paydays from monthly to fortnightly can be winning factors when it comes to clinching the deal.

Undercover and undaunted

In spite of all the obstacles I was encountering, I stuck with my temping role because it was such a fascinating experiment. I could also see what a difference my new recruits were making to the line managers. The carpentry supervisor was so excited by the change that he told the CFO how fabulous he was finding the 'new recruitment process'. He didn't know that the CFO hadn't authorised it in the first place or that she didn't even know what the process was.

When I asked him what his own interview had been like he told me it had been pretty bad. 'Emma, the payroll girl, just went through a list of questions from A to Z and ticked off each answer on her clipboard,' he said. 'I only took the role because I love yachts and I really wanted to work on them. If it had been any other job I would have run a mile.'

His next comment was also revealing. 'Some of my mates applied too. They didn't take the job because they didn't like her. She put them off with her manner.'

Bone 5: dedicated, skilled, practised recruiters

This is typical of many organisations. They use unskilled, low-level staff to recruit, even though all the evidence points to the fact that the quality of the hirer plays a big part in the recruitment outcome.

The top 5 ingredients of a successful recruiter

Here are my top 5 ingredients for a great recruiter.

1 *Sales skills.* The recruiter must be one of the organisation's best salespeople to attract and employ the best people for the business. A clear understanding of and enthusiasm for the organisation and the advertised role, and a real ability to sell the benefits to prospective candidates are key requirements.

2 *Demonstrated high achievement.* Like attracts like and highfliers attract other highfliers. They inspire applicants with the story of their own journey, which makes the candidate more likely to accept a job offer, and they're confident enough to employ applicants who may be superior to them in ability or skills. Small companies do this naturally because often it's the owner doing the recruiting. This is why achievers who have come up through the ranks of an organisation can make the best recruiters. The reverse is also true. One organisation I worked with relocated its failed sales staff into administrative roles. A number of them ended up as recruiters (because hiring was treated as an administrative area) and the quality of new recruits deteriorated.

3 *Communication and coaching skills.* Recruiters need good communication skills to deal with applicants and internal stakeholders, especially as there's always a lot of pressure to fill positions. Coaching techniques are useful because they influence internal staff to make good decisions without being dictatorial. An example would be asking a manager a coaching question such as, 'This person may have the right skills but they have a 75 per cent risk of turnover because they haven't lasted in a single job for longer than 12 months. What would be the impact to your team if they left within the next few months?' The manager can make an

(continued)

The top 5 ingredients of a successful recruiter (cont'd)

objective final decision, albeit with all the information at hand. Compare the effect of this question to a typical 'telling' instruction, such as, 'You can't employ this person because they've failed the company testing'.

4   *A people-friendly focus.* People would rather do something for someone they like than someone they don't like. Warm, empathic recruiters fill positions.

5   *Practice, practice, practice.* Recruitment is not an exact science so the best way for recruiters to improve what they do is through experiential learning. This is why dedicated recruiters who are focused on the discipline are a better option than someone who might recruit only a few times per year, such as a line manager. It's also why an HR degree is not vital to being a great recruiter. In some cases it can even be a handicap if an individual gets too fixated on conventional systems and processes.

Employing high-achieving, motivated recruiters can have more impact on hiring success than just about any other single factor.

Bone 6: a generous, merit-based salary and effective measurement

Of course, attracting and keeping talented recruiters means paying them a decent salary. Teresa's people were being paid half of a reasonable recruiter's wage so it wasn't surprising that the corresponding return on investment was also low. Good recruiters hire quickly and efficiently, reduce staff turnover and enable a company to achieve its business goals. These savings far exceed the cost of any salary investment.

Teresa's HR area also had no method for measuring the effectiveness of its recruiters, no useful data that helped improve hiring practices, and no compelling statistics for changing HR understanding and strategies at the executive level. Not only does this lead to inertia, but it can also be actively damaging to a business.

For instance, one of my clients told me he was thinking about sacking Sean, his recruiter, because of anecdotal evidence from his store managers about poor communication skills. 'Compared to Bronwyn [his other recruiter], who was a renowned hirer, each month topping the honour board of most new recruits, he's just not cutting it,' he told me. When we looked at real data for three months, however, we found that Sean's retention rate of new people was 85 per cent and every single one had achieved their sales targets. In stark contrast, 19 out of 21 of Bronwyn's new recruits had left in their first three months, so her retention rate was only 10 per cent. No-one had known this, not even Bronwyn herself, because the only data the company collected and reported on was vacancies filled. The CEO was shocked. He'd nearly sacked his best recruiter!

What gets measured gets managed

Here are some of the other things I measure:

- The cost of running the HR area.
- The cost of HR initiatives.
- The cost of recruitment advertising.
- The percentage success of recruitment advertising.
- Positions vacant.
- Positions filled.
- The recruitment conversion rate.
- The speed of recruitment from ad placement to job offer.
- The retention of recruits.
- The new recruit's performance (for measurable positions such as sales).
- The cost of staff turnover.
- The profit increase of increased retention.

I always compare these figures to the overall company results, as per the Key Performance Indicator sheet in figure 2.1 (overleaf) so that executives can see the true ramifications of their recruitment practices, the return on investment (ROI) and how this relates back to profit.

Figure 2.1: recruitment success indicators

Recruitment success indicators

KPI	YEAR	JUL	AUG	SEP	OCT	NOV	DEC	JAN	FEB	MAR	APR	MAY	JUN	Total yr end	Running average
Company staff turnover															
Total no. of staff	2013														
	2014														
	2015														
No. of staff turnover	2013														
	2014														
	2015														
Month % staff turnover	2013														
	2014														
	2015														
Annualised % staff turnover	2013														
	2014														
	2015														
Cost of staff turnover $45 000 (50% annual average salary)	2013														
	2014														
	2015														
Recruitment area success															
Total no. vacancies	2013														
	2014														
	2015														
No. good CVs received	2013														
	2014														
	2015														
Vacancies filled	2013														
	2014														
	2015														

% vacancies filled	2013									
	2014									
	2015									
Recruitment conversion rate	2013									
	2014									
	2015									
Recruitment area finances										
Income from fees charged per new recruit (can be notional)	2013									
	2014									
	2015									
Advertising costs	2013									
	2014									
	2015									
Total area costs, incl. advertising	2013									
	2014									
	2015									
Net profit/loss	2013									
	2014									
	2015									
Overall Company Impact										
Company profit	2013									
	2014									
	2015									
% Cost of staff turnover to profit	2013									
	2014									
	2015									
% Recruitment area costs to profit	2013									
	2014									
	2015									

Measuring success in this way is always a great motivator and one guaranteed to get the chief's attention.

Crossing the finish line

By the end of the month I'd recruited 28 people for the yachting company. Teresa asked me to stay on and doubled my temp wage to $44 an hour. I agreed to work for two more weeks and recruited another 21 people. By this time we'd reduced the recruitment spend by $10 000 per week and I'd filled more than half of the total vacancies. I didn't want to finish as I was on such a roll, but I had a commitment with Australia's Bond University so it was time to go.

On my last day the company organised a goodbye cake and the factory staff came to share it with me. I felt a real sense of achievement. I'd evolved some of the company's HR practices, relieved much of their employment burden, enabled them to retrieve two multimillion-dollar contracts and encouraged the line managers to take ownership of their own people and problems.

I'd also seen firsthand what happens when the bones of recruitment (see below) aren't in place. Number 1 is the most crucial. With a positive attitude, any organisation—whether it's a two-person business or a global corporation—can make the continuous improvements necessary to achieve hiring success. Without it, a company has almost no chance of improving its recruitment results. The revolutionary process of 'un-education'—replacing conventional methods with proven strategies that deliver consistently good results—can't happen without input, engagement and buy-in from people at all levels of the company.

The six bones of great recruitment

Applying these six bones will ensure hiring success.

1   A positive and proactive corporate attitude towards recruitment.

2   An HR champion with direct access to the company leader.

3   Involvement of the line managers in some form in the recruitment process.

The six bones of great recruitment *(cont'd)*

4 The alignment of business practices with good recruitment outcomes.

5 Dedicated, skilled and practised recruiter/s.

6 A generous, merit-based recruiter salary and effective measurement.

Like a skeleton, the bones only work in conjunction with each other. For instance, involving line managers in the recruitment process without the assistance of a dedicated, skilled and practised recruiter (who may be from a recruitment agency if the company has no-one with skills in this area) leads to poor-fit employees and a high staff turnover. Skip one bone and the rest disconnect and are ineffective.

My stint at the yachting company also taught me that it's possible to achieve short-term hiring success without all the bones in place. Long-term, however, it's unsustainable. My efforts had been like a short shock treatment. Once I left, the company could easily revert to its traditional habits. If it didn't reform any of its business practices, there was a real risk that the good people I'd employed would turn over and the whole cycle of rising vacancies would begin once again. Yet I had to accept that this was out of my hands. My boatbuilding career was over.

The final outcome

Several years later, I went online to see how the yachting company was faring. I was saddened, but not surprised, to learn that it had gone into liquidation. I wondered how much its poor hiring processes and people systems had contributed to its demise. Many organisations don't recognise that recruitment is a key piston in their engine and if it's broken the additional stress it puts on all other aspects of the business is enormous. Maybe this wasn't the case here. But with one million dollars annually wasted on recruitment advertising, the loss of multimillion-dollar contracts through inadequate staffing, and the massive staff turnover and resultant stress caused by the corporation's focus on bureaucracy, rather than people, I suspect that maybe it was.

The six bones of great recruitment

Answer the following questions to determine whether your organisation has the critical bones of great recruitment in place.

→ Does our organisation have a positive and proactive corporate attitude towards recruitment?

→ Do we have an HR champion as an influential part of the senior leadership team and/or with direct access to the company leader?

→ Are our line managers involved in the recruitment process, in some form?

→ Do we constantly improve our business practices to align with good recruitment outcomes?

→ Who are our current recruiters and are they focused on recruitment?

→ Does each one have the five ingredients necessary to be a great recruiter?

→ Do they get continuous practice in recruitment?

→ Are they paid a decent salary?

→ Can they influence and make changes to business practices that impact on retention?

→ Are they measured and rewarded for effectiveness?

→ Do we have objective recruitment KPIs in place that relate to overall company results?

CHAPTER 3

Attracting: what great people want and how to sell it to them

When it is obvious that the goals cannot be reached,
don't adjust the goals, adjust the action steps.

Confucius, Chinese philosopher

I knew my recruitment marketing was having an impact in the UK when my company was featured in a popular British lifestyle magazine. In an entrapment-style scam, the editor sent me the application of a girl called Geraldine Halliwell to see if I would employ her as a travel agent. She had an A level in English, but since leaving school she'd been a nightclub dancer, a glamour model and was now a member of an unnamed band. Her greatest talents were identified as singing and dancing, but as her résumé didn't show any success in these fields, I put her on my 'no' pile. I found out that I'd knocked back Ginger Spice—from the legendary Spice Girls pop band—when I read about it in the headline of a newspaper.

At the time this article was published, we only had about twelve stores in London so I figured to be chosen by the scammers meant that our tiny recruitment ad in *The Sunday Times* really stood out. And it did. As we highlighted that we were looking for proven achievers *in any field*, while our rivals were still focused on traditional job skills, our ad was like a beacon in the marketplace. This is crucial for attracting great recruits. When people complain that 'there simply aren't any good candidates out there', I often find the real reason is that they're inept at attracting people.

Take Paul, the CEO of a large national retailer, who rang me because he wanted help hiring an area manager. He'd been advertising for two months but hadn't had one decent application. When I asked him what he'd written in his ad it was standard stuff: job title, salary, role description, and education and experience required. It was clear that his ad was centred around selection criteria.

'And how did you sell the job role?' I asked. 'What benefits did you include?'

There was a pause. 'Just the salary,' he admitted. 'I didn't really think about it much. It's a management role and we're well known so I thought I'd be fighting people off for this position.'

Paul was a savvy guy, but he'd omitted a crucial step in attraction:

Think about what the candidate wants.

In the middle of a skills shortage, he'd failed to stand out from the pack by showing the concrete benefits of working for his organisation. There were some decent candidates out there. He just hadn't attracted the attention of any of them with his conventional advertising. He wasn't selling the position.

Selling rather than screening

Paul's approach is quite normal. Pick up any newspaper careers section or look on any online sites and the majority of job ads are based around selection criteria. Because applicants have outnumbered vacancies for nearly 100 years, the focus of recruiters has long been on screening, rather than attracting, because this ensured that only people with the specific advertised criteria made it through to an interview. The onus was on them to excel in the recruitment process if they wanted to get the job, and there was no need for employers to generate excitement about a role.

Twenty-first-century hiring requires a corporate mental flip. The *employer* must now excel at the recruitment process and be proactive to capture the attention of great potential candidates and to encourage them to apply. *Then* they can screen the unsuitable ones out. It's Sales 101 again. Great organisations now accept that the only way they'll attract enough of the right sort of people to achieve their business growth is by identifying candidates' needs, looking at how they can meet them and then using targeted marketing to advertise to these prospects a compelling package of benefits.

What candidates want

So what should go into this package? If you ask people the hypothetical question 'What do you want in a job?' many will reply 'money'. However, if you ask them *after* they've taken a role what motivated them to do so, it's almost never money. In fact, in the numerous published rankings of the 10 conditions that have the most impact on employee motivation, money usually falls between fifth and tenth on the list.

This is common sense. If the job location doesn't suit, work hours are too long or conditions are poor, no amount of money will compensate. That's why mining companies struggle to find staff for their remote sites, despite offering record salaries.

I saw another great example of this in June 2007 when managers of a rural medical practice in remote Australia offered a 500 000-dollar lump sum to any GP, anaesthetist or obstetrician who was willing to move there from the city.[7] The money would be paid after the completion of a three-month probationary period and was in addition to the more than 200 000-dollar annual salary. Despite the fact that the offer made national and international headlines, with the story being reported as far afield as France and the UK, there were no takers.

Money by itself, then, is not the greatest motivator, and employers who try to attract candidates using salary alone may be successful in the short-term but guarantee themselves high staff turnover. The same goes for organisations that use gimmicks such as iPhones to prop up recruitment, which is a poor long-term retention strategy. The only thing new recruits will use their new iPhones for is to take calls for interviews from future employers.

To attract and retain the best long-term recruits then, employers must look at a number of elements, in addition to money, to create an irresistible combination. I've trialled and tested a lot of ideas on this front and here are the most successful factors that I've found attract people to a position.

Time

Because of the pressure of work, time is now a commodity. Despite technological improvements, work hours are escalating in many developed countries, so control over and flexibility in scheduling time are becoming more and more valuable, and many people are prepared to take a lower salary as a trade-off. It's not surprising then, that companies that embed time flexibility into their organisational make-up, and sell this concept in their recruitment marketing, experience outstanding success.

Take the Marriott Hotel group, which was looking for great people to staff its new hotel in Hong Kong. The company discovered a six-day work week was standard there, so they implemented an attractive five-day work week and filled all their positions with employees of their choice.

My local bus company was also having difficulty hiring new drivers as most of their prospective recruits had been swallowed up by the booming Australian mining companies. After focusing on the needs of their target market, the organisation created a new shift time from 9.30 am to 2.30 pm, and filled all their vacancies with parents who wanted to only work between school hours.

St George Bank identified that many of their prospective employees wanted time to pursue other interests without sacrificing their careers. The bank attracted more recruits by introducing a policy that let employees work four years and take a fifth year off, fully paid.

It worked like this: if an employee's annual salary was $50 000, they were paid $40 000 for four years and then, when they took the fifth year off, they were paid $40 000, which was made up of the $10 000 owing from each of the previous four years. This is great creative salary packaging, makes a real point of difference and the icing on the cake is that because employees lock in for five years, staff turnover is reduced.

Telecommuting is another way to give employees more time because they cut down on commuting hours. The rise of the internet has increased the ability of mainstream organisations to offer this option. Multiple award-winning US airline company Jet Blue, for instance, employs 700 reservation agents and they all work from home. The company has 30 per cent higher productivity and much lower staff turnover than other airlines.

Some organisations still see telecommuting as an excuse for people to laze around. Yet all the latest studies show a statistical increase in productivity when employees work from home. One longitudinal study, in which psychologists examined 20 years of research on telecommuting involving 46 studies and 12 833 employees, found that it has an overall beneficial effect and is a win–win for both employees and employers, resulting in higher morale and job satisfaction and lower employee stress and turnover.[8]

Often those who are the most fervent in blaming telecommuting for their bottom line woes, have poor metrics and management processes. Moving demotivated, unproductive workers from home to office is like relocating rotten apples and expecting them to taste fresh. If organisations have objective measurements in place for employee outcomes, then managers can identify and deal with poor performers, no matter where their workplace.

And let's not lose sight of reality. The number of organisations that allow their employees to work at least part of their regular paid hours at home has almost doubled since 2005[9], so employers such as Yahoo, whose new CEO banned employees from working from home in 2013, are losing a real competitive edge in the war for talent. Axing telecommuting at a time when more and more good people are calling for increased flexibility doesn't take into account the true cost of these types of changes either. I'd be amazed if this kind of blanket, all-roles, non–family friendly policy didn't increase staff turnover, which as I've said, can often be a company's greatest hidden expense.

Finally, one of the best time-saving innovations is when corporations offer their employees in-house amenities that they would normally have to source for themselves out of hours. For instance, Google employees at the company's Mountain View headquarters can access onsite oil-change and car-wash services, a doctor and a chiropractor, dry cleaning, massage therapy, a gym, a hair stylist, fitness classes and bike-repair facilities. Smaller businesses that can't afford to provide these kinds of services in-house can create a list of out-sourced contractors who offer discounted onsite services at the employees' expense. This resource then becomes another sales tool to give the employer an edge over competitors. I'll talk more about these kinds of perks in chapter 7.

Brightness of future (BOF)

I asked every person I interviewed why they were looking to leave their existing employer. More than 75 per cent of them replied that it was because they couldn't see any future with the organisation. Many liked their company and/or their manager but there was simply nowhere left for them to go; no way for them to grow and develop; no 'brightness of future'.

By identifying, offering and advertising specific BOF selling points in recruitment ads, employers can target and attract excellent applicants, many of whom might be disengaged from their companies, but not actively job seeking. For instance, every recruitment ad I placed included the words, 'We promote 99 per cent from within', which attracted many disgruntled applicants whose companies recruited external applicants for their senior roles.

Here are some BOF elements that I've used successfully in advertising:

- Promotional opportunities.
- Rapid growth of an organisation or job area and/or any fast-track schemes.

- Rewards and recognition programs.

- Overseas assignments and secondments and other corporate travel opportunities.

- Job security or factors that show longevity/stability of the organisation (this has become more important following some of the spectacular corporate failures during the GFC).

- Distinctive training/mentoring programs that are outside the norm.

- Company awards or innovations.

A role that engages

This is one of the great candidate attractors and yet it is rarely used in recruitment advertising. I applied the principle unconsciously for years, without ever understanding how or why it worked. It wasn't until I read Frederick Herzberg's best-selling book *The Motivation to Work*[10] that I began to comprehend why I had some friends who never left dreadful companies and why others quit from what to all intents and purposes were excellent organisations.

Herzberg conducted a large-scale study of worker motivation in the US in 1959 and discovered that employees rated achievement in the actual job itself as their biggest motivator at work. This included such aspects as doing creative, challenging and varied work; the opportunity to do a job completely from beginning to end; working without supervision; and being responsible for one's own efforts. Salary, interpersonal relationships, company policy and working conditions were all inferior to these factors.

Now I understood why one of my friends kept working for an appalling employer. His actual job was diverse and interesting so he just ignored the political in-fighting and dysfunctionality that surrounded him. The same principle applied to the ones who quit from exciting organisations. Their tangible job role simply wasn't engaging enough.

I realised that I could apply this principle to attraction. If I analysed every role I needed to fill and advertised the positive qualities of the actual job itself, not just of the organisation, I could draw in more of my desired applicants and improve my recruitment success. This is exactly what happened. When I was called in to recruit for a company manager, the position had been advertised before and had attracted no suitable applicants. After delving deeply to understand the job role, we added just one word—autonomy—and soon filled the position with one of more than 10 suitable people who applied.

The same thing happened when I was asked to recruit cabinetmakers for a fit-out company. It was standard practice for them to work on one component, such as drawers, and then pass their work on to the next cabinetmaker to add to. By advertising the fact that the role we were advertising involved working on the fit-out from start to end and being responsible for the total finished product, we were inundated with good applicants.

To be inspired

Many longitudinal studies show that employees want to work for organisations that have a clear direction and purpose. They want to be engaged and enthused beyond the bland mission statement or generic goal of financial returns. In practice, I've found that the addition of a compelling recruitment vision—separate from the corporate vision—has a big impact on applications and candidate interest.

Here's one of my favourites. It's from Gore, the company behind GORE-TEX®, which at the time of writing had made it onto *Fortune* magazine's '100 Best Companies to Work For' list for 14 consecutive years and had annual sales of US$25 billion dollars:

> *Discover how a Gore team developed a device that changes the way doctors treat patients with serious heart defects. Discover how a Gore team invented a guitar string that inspires musicians to play. Discover how a Gore team engineered high performance fabrics that change the way fire fighters respond to emergencies. If you are searching for a company where you can have an impact and make a difference, we're looking for you! What can you change by joining Gore?*

Every time I read this I want to go and work for Gore. It's much more engaging than if the company just outlined that they produce fabrics, medical devices, electronics and manufacturing, and it's certainly better than the old chestnut, 'People are our best asset'. It also sends a strong message to candidates: 'We're looking for achievement-oriented people who want to make a difference'. Those who respond to this message are more likely to be high quality and a good match for the company's cultural requirements.

Of course, a recruitment vision must be *genuine* to be effective. Otherwise people will leave when their expectations don't match the reality. This is a common mistake. Organisations often get so into 'marketing-speak' that they let the truth fly out the window. 'People are our greatest asset' is a cliché I often see on mission statements that has very little practical application.

'Work–life balance' is another repeat offender. One of my clients had this as an integral part of their vision, yet their position descriptions stated: 'Applicants are on call 24 hours a day, 7 days a week'. It was a real mismatch of ideals and one that led to constant staff turnover when the person attracted by the work–life balance discovered that it didn't exist at all. This is typical of many companies that treat applicants as though they're stupid and then wonder why they have such massive drop-out rates. The widespread use of social media also means that these disillusioned recruits can influence a lot of other great potential candidates too.

The choice of selection criteria also has a big impact on the quality of applicants. Some act as inspiring attractors in their own right. For instance, when I asked for 'demonstrated achievement' in my ad, I tripled the number of applications from suitable candidates. Saying that a tertiary degree, or a 'demonstrated commitment to continuous improvement and learning' would be 'desirable' had a similar impact, albeit a bit less powerful. My theory is that these kinds of criteria act as a proactive flag to people with great attitudes and ability, and motivate them to apply.

The reverse is also true. I have found that some criteria are detrimental to recruitment success. For instance, in Paul's ad he'd asked for someone with three years' experience. It made me wonder how many great candidates he'd missed out on who had only had 2-and-three-quarter years of experience. The problem with using years of experience as a key screening factor is that it doesn't take merit into account. All Paul really needed was someone who had actual demonstrated achievement in this field, with applicable work examples as proof. Whether they'd worked for two years or 20 years was irrelevant.

Points of difference

Once an organisation has considered what people want and has assessed its own practices, it can create a compelling package that highlights all the benefits for prospective candidates (as shown in figure 3.1). It's these points of difference—which many HR books refer to as the employee value proposition (EVP)—that give an organisation a real edge in the job marketplace. As well as the above motivators this also includes organisation-specific selling points such as a unique marketing niche, an innovative employee-focused workplace design or external recognition.

Figure 3.1: example of an attractor package

Position-specific	Organisation-specific
➢ Autonomous role	➢ Winner *Times* 'Small Business Award' 2011
➢ Flexible work hours with the ability to work from home part-time	➢ One of *BRW*'s 'Top 500 Fastest Growing Companies'
➢ Attractive CBD location, including car park, close to shops and restaurants	➢ Innovative work practices with major clients including X, Y
➢ Start-up position so exceptional potential for career growth	
➢ Salary and generous merit-based incentive structure (OTE $100 000)	

Creating a package that people will want takes time and thought. It can also involve confronting some brutal facts. Often my clients have no obvious, identifiable candidate attractors or they can't compete with market salaries, so I always start with a reality check. If a corporation can't identify any points of difference, then it needs to create some. Once a business gets past its own blinkered thinking it's amazing how many opportunities there are in this area, such as modifying job roles, altering shift times or introducing telecommuting in some job roles, even if it's just for one day a week or fortnight.

Here's another key to effective attraction:

Change business practices to create compelling attractors.

Once again, this can't be done without an HR champion who has direct influence at the executive level: someone who can persuade the executives that to fill positions, cut staff turnover by 'x' per cent and create savings in the millions of dollars, these modifications are vital.

Raving fans within

Placing the applicant and their needs at the centre of business practices is also important for another reason. Take Sam, a termite inspector, who shared a coffee with me after he'd checked the foundations of my house. When I asked him about his work he said, 'Actually I'm trying to get another job'.

I asked him why.

'My boss is a real a★★★hole,' he said. 'He never pays me on time, he yells at all the staff and he always rings me to do work on my time off, and expects me to cancel whatever I'm doing. And when I do come in, I never even get a thank you!'

Everyone has met a disgruntled employee. Most of us have probably been one at some stage and we wouldn't take much notice of this rant. If I were a job-seeker, however, and I'd met three people from this organisation who all thought that the termite boss was an a★★★hole, I'd run a mile from applying for a position. This is why placing people's needs at the centre of the business is so important to recruitment. There's no point spending thousands of dollars on recruitment advertising if anyone who asks existing employees what they think of the organisation is going to get a litany of complaints.

The 'raving fans within' concept is a term I borrowed and adapted from a popular sales book,[11] and it's crucial to effective hiring. If employees are engaged and enthusiastic, they will function like an organisation's best recruiters, spreading the word within their own social circles. The reverse is also true. Unhappy, demotivated people such as Sam repel good applicants with their stories of poor business methods and mismanagement.

It is important, then, that companies have active strategies in place so that their own people become raving fans within, and this again comes back to business practices. There are many ways to do this, such as reducing unnecessary paperwork; designing a rewards and recognition program; implementing more flexible job-sharing and leave options; creating family-friendly policies; organising regular fun social events; axing incompetent managers; initiating staff feedback surveys and—more critically—acting on them; enhancing transparency and communication; and promoting more people from within. Practices such as these create a powerful cycle in which great new recruits are attracted, become raving fans themselves and attract more good candidates.

Once an organisation has a 'raving fans' culture in place, they can be proactive about hiring. One retailer I worked with produced recruitment postcards and gave a box to every employee to hand out to friends or salespeople they met when they were out shopping, who they thought would be great for the business. They then paid each staff member $1000 when the person they had referred was hired. This was much cheaper than paying a recruitment agency or placing repeated ads. As an added advantage, they also found that the individuals they recruited through employee referrals had lower turnover than other groups because, after having talked to someone face to face, they had a better understanding of the business, warts and all, before they even started.

The corporate website: an inspiring online presence

Before an organisation begins to advertise any positions, it needs an effective careers website. When a recruitment ad catches an applicant's interest, the company's website is often their first port of call, so it's essential that the front page of the site is a powerful selling tool. By expanding on the objective benefits of working for the company, the website can target the candidate 'wants', as identified in the first step of the attraction process. An inspiring recruitment vision on this page also acts as a major attractor to potential recruits.

Career websites that use social media to build better relationships with prospective candidates are also proving popular and are a valuable tool for measurement as well, due to the detailed analytics of users. Unscripted raving fans' comments posted online can increase the attraction value for other candidates and questions posted are a great way to expose weaknesses that can be beefed up for future advertised vacancies.

Selling the benefits in the job ad

Once an organisation has worked out its points of difference, it is also ready to begin recruiting. Creating a successful job ad is the first and most important step in this process. Think of it as an arrow flying through the air. A well-thought-out ad outlining an organisation's points of difference hits the target, galvanises suitable candidates to apply for a role and increases the statistical probability of recruitment success.

Despite this, recruiters often rush out ads with little thought. Even though a departing employee may have given them four weeks' notice, many leave the hiring process until right before they need the replacement. Then they give it minimal attention and end up with cliché-ridden drivel such as these actual examples, which I found in a quick trawl of a major job search website:

> *'Amist (sic) the suspense, the drama & the intrigue is an opportunity to keep the chase alive & the chase is still on for a Regional Guru to join this co.!!'*
>
> *'Cool, Committed, Caring, Innovative, Exciting and Energetic? We want you to come on board the starship!'*
>
> *'This retail outfit knows their business with their finger firmly planted on the trend pulse & with no signs of slowing down!!'*

This type of descriptive, criteria-led advertising is endemic and wastes a lot of time and money. A poor ad makes a bad first impression and doesn't attract suitable applicants, but it takes weeks of screening CVs and interviewing to work this out. Then the organisation is forced to re-advertise and begin the whole process again.

By now their recruitment prospects are damaged because positions that are re-advertised create an even worse impression. They make the organisation appear desperate for applicants, when in fact a poor ad was the problem. By now the recruiter and the organisation *are* getting desperate to fill the position so they're more likely to lower their criteria and appoint a sub-standard recruit. This inevitably leads to low productivity and future staff turnover and then the whole wretched cycle starts again.

Creating an effective job ad

Here's my list of factors that guarantee success when putting together a job ad.

- *Use only specific, objective facts.* Clichés and vague statements have no real meaning to good applicants and do not inspire them to apply. Compare, 'This brand is fast, furious and not for the faint-hearted' with 'Company X opens a new business operation every three months and promotes 99 per cent from within', which is far more effective. Selection criteria should also be specific and measurable. Don't join together a string of meaningless platitudes such as, 'Cool, Committed, Caring, Innovative, Exciting and Energetic'.

- *Sell the benefits of the organisation and the job role at the top of the ad.* It's not enough to come up with what people want; you also have to make these attractors prominent so people see them in the first few seconds of skimming through job ads. When there are only a few suitable applicants in the marketplace an organisation has to capture the attention of as many of them as possible.

- *Always put an indicative salary in the ad.* I have road-tested this for many years and found that I get twice as many suitable applicants when I include an indicative remuneration guide such as 'generous salary and bonuses OTE $75 000 +' (where OTE means 'on target earnings'). Keith, a marketing expert I once worked with, often said, 'If it hasn't got a price, it ain't for sale' and research backs this up, showing that customers are more likely to enter a shop if the price of products is displayed outside. Including a salary in the ad works in the same way, although I don't usually include the exact base wage for roles that are negotiable. This technique also saves a lot of time and energy screening and interviewing unsuitable recruits as people earning $200000 won't mistakenly apply for roles offering only $50000, and vice versa. Being inundated with applicants is not a good result—it's the number of suitable ones that counts.

- *Use the company logo in every recruitment ad.* If an organisation has a strong brand this is a real plus in attracting potential candidates because people like to know where they are applying. Often logos are not used because marketers are almost never involved in HR advertising, even though filling staff vacancies may be the company's biggest challenge. Similarly, if an organisation is outsourcing to a recruitment agency, they should include their logo in the advertising, unless confidentiality is deemed an issue.

- *Use a separate ad for each job and categorise them correctly.* Some employers try to save money by writing a consolidated ad with multi-jobs and then plonking it into one section in the media or on a job-search website. This is the equivalent of trying to sell cans of baked beans in an office furniture shop. It's also false economy because it ends up costing employers more in re-advertising when they miss their target market, who only read the careers sections specific to their job.

Positioning the ad in its appropriate category is also vital. One of my clients advertised for a global recruitment leader in the 'Recruitment—Internal' category on a job-search site and didn't receive a single suitable applicant. When we re-advertised using the 'Management—Internal' section they received at least eight applicants who were a good fit for the role.

Figure 3.2 (overleaf) shows an ad that demonstrates all these factors. If I want to place this in an expensive medium, I can also run a very small ad that just uses the header and the employee benefits, and then direct applicants to a webpage with more selling points and selection criteria for them to read at their leisure.

Figure 3.2: a benefits-led recruitment ad

	Innovative E-learning Designer
Role description →	
Key attractions →	**Use your creative flair and design expertise to build a revolutionary new learning system and enjoy autonomy, flexible work hours and an $80K+ package.**
Selling points of company →	Acme is one of the country's largest _____ organisations and the winner of the *Times Small Business Award 2011*. Its phenomenal growth since start-up, has earned it *BRW* magazine's 'Fastest Growing Company' title and its innovative practices have led to it winning such major contracts as _____ project, _____ and _____, among others.
Inspiring outcomes-based role overview →	Acme is looking to employ a creative designer to transform its people processes by taking content and turning it into exciting, interactive IT solutions. You will be responsible for sourcing, designing, applying and managing innovative multi-media solutions as well as researching and implementing an effective learning management system. This is a unique, exciting opportunity to help build an integrated people system that is fun, engaging and inspires Acme's teams around Australia.
Employee benefits →	**Benefits include:** • Autonomy to create cutting-edge solutions. • Flexible work hours with the ability to work from home part-time. • Salary and generous merit-based incentive structure (OTE $80 000). • Start-up position so exceptional potential for career growth. • Attractive CBD location including car park, close to shops and restaurants.
Criteria to motivate high achievers to apply →	**Selection criteria:** • Tertiary degree in any discipline desirable. • Demonstrated achievement in this field. • Existing portfolio of innovative multi-media design. • Experience in delivering creative IT solutions to achieve effective outcomes, on time and within budget. • Excellent verbal, written and interpersonal communication. • A demonstrated commitment to continuous improvement and learning.
Wrap-up →	An immediate start is on offer so if you are seeking a genuine career opportunity and would like to be a crucial member of Acme's team to build an inspiring workplace, this exciting role is for you. Send your CV and a cover letter to ....
Branding with logo →	**LOGO**

The ad as a template

It does and should take time for a recruiter to produce the first ad of this kind. I usually spend at least a day working out an organisation's points of difference and then it takes me hours to put together an effective ad. Like writing a short story, I mull over it and tinker with it over a few days, or even a week. Then I give it to three or four people in the organisation for reviewing so I can improve it.

Once a new ad is in place, however, it saves hours of work because it can be used as a template for the organisation's future ads. The organisation's points of difference stay the same and the recruiter simply slots in the benefits, selection criteria and role description for each position. This means no matter what time pressure the recruiter is under, the job ad is always professional, consistent and effective, and can be rolled out with speed. The ad also becomes a means for ongoing innovation because by changing a single factor and measuring the increase or decrease of the now standard level of response, it can be continually improved.

Recruitment marketing: measure, measure, measure

For roles that don't require any specialised skills, recruitment marketing is easy because advertising on any of the leading online job-search sites will usually attract the right people. Yet many employers still trawl lots of different marketing avenues, even for these basic positions. When I dig down, I often discover this is because they don't have a decent attractor package or sales-focused ad. It's like they're trying to catch a fish with no bait on the hook, so they compensate by flinging their net in everywhere.

Recruiting for more specialised, senior or high-demand positions is a more challenging proposition and this is where employers often go astray. It's not surprising really. There are many avenues for recruitment advertising, all of which profess to be tremendously effective. Misinformation is rife and as positions become harder to fill, organisations become more vulnerable to snake-oil salespeople.

I'm not a marketing guru, but I do understand one thing: an ad is only as good as the response it generates in terms of quality and volume. When I first started recruiting, newspaper careers sections were the dominant medium. Because there were many different publications, I learned that to be effective I needed to measure the result of every single ad placed. By doing this, within a few months I had objective information about where my most successful candidates came from, which I then used in my next round of hiring.

Using this approach, I discovered in the early days of internet job-search sites that compared with other media advertising I received about twenty times the number of responses, yet only about one-tenth of my successful recruits came from them (see table 3.1). This flood of bad applicants took a lot of time and energy to process, with little return. Without an effective measurement system I would never have known that this was such a poor option.

Table 3.1: recruitment marketing effectiveness KPI

Position: cabinetmaker Number required: 10 Campaign start date: 14 June				
Advertising source	**Newspaper**	**Job-search website**	**Radio**	**Total**
Ad spend	$1500	$750	$550	$2800
Number of CVs received	45	280	25	350
Number of suitable CVs	15	4	4	23
Number of candidates interviewed	15	4	3	22
Number of candidates employed	8	1	1	10
Cost per recruit	$188	$750	$550	$149
% interviewed*	33.33%	1.4%	12%	15.9%
Recruitment conversion rate^	53%	25%	25%	43%

* Number interviewed divided by number of CVs received
^ Number employed divided by number suitable

These statistics are changing constantly, but the soaring recruitment marketing options made possible by technical advances and the rise of social media and networking sites such as LinkedIn, Twitter, Facebook and Google Plus makes this kind of objective assessment even more essential. There are hundreds of books and blogs written on this subject so I'll keep my comments short. Here are my tips for recruitment marketing in the twenty-first century.

- *Be proactive and get educated.* Read books and subscribe to web feeds, newsletters and specialty websites that give you the latest information on recruitment marketing apps and innovations. Or book in a consultation with one of the many innovative marketing companies springing up that offer advice to time-poor, techno-unsavvy businesspeople. Education is the first step in making informed choices.

- *Analyse the evidence for hiring success.* There's a lot of hype about new technologies and social media applications, but don't get excited without positive proof. Despite what gung-ho marketers tell you, the reality is that some of these advances will be effective and others lemons, and the only way to tell will be by analysing existing evidence. Ask probing questions such as:

  - Who has used this technique previously?

  - What have been the *objective* hiring benefits?

  - Is it cost- and time-effective?

  - Does it create a great applicant impression?

  - Can I talk to some existing users?

- *Fire bullets, not cannonballs.* In some instances of recruitment marketing, the technology will be so new that there is *no* evidence as to its effectiveness. The book *Great by Choice*, a study of companies that have demonstrated long-term business success, outlines how a 'fire bullets, then cannonballs' approach is better than 'big-leap innovations and predictive genius'[12] in this type of scenario.

  A bullet is a low-cost, low-risk test to empirically validate what will work. It is used to trial and measure ideas before deciding on implementation. Using the bullets approach, an HR leader doesn't have to be a visionary genius. They just fire a significant number of bullets every year to determine which marketing avenues will be most successful. Based on that empirical validation, they then consolidate their resources to fire a single cannonball, enabling large returns from concentrated bets.

Unfortunately, many companies approach new technology with all cannons ablaze. One firm I talked to was very excited about its new, expensive careers website, which allowed applicants to link in using all forms of social media. When I analysed the evidence, it hadn't increased hiring success in any way—that is, filled vacancies and staff turnover were still the same as before, and it was costing the business an extra $60 000 a year in wages for a full-time employee to respond to the tsunami of postings. Unfortunately, because they'd expended so much money on this new system, the business was wedded to it and had no budget left to use for alternative, more effective marketing approaches.

- *Head-hunt achievers in existing roles through networks and professional communities.* Some of the best recruits are people who are not actively job-seeking. Unfortunately many job-search sites only link to registered enquirers, and the demise of Saturday newspaper careers sections—which attracted casual browsers—has taken head-hunting to a new level of difficulty. Employers now have to be far more proactive if they want to target skilled employees in entrenched roles. Recruitment advertising that directly targets members of online business networks and specialty communities, paying for professional email lists and keeping in contact with specialist head-hunters are a few steps in resolving this modern dilemma.

It's important to keep up-to-date on the subject of recruitment marketing, but don't get side-tracked in the process and don't spend all your time on it. This is only one step in the whole hiring process. It's important to get it right, but it's not the *only* step that's important. Companies that focus solely on attraction and don't improve other aspects of their hiring processes will never experience long-term recruitment success.

What if you still can't fill a vacancy?

The killer scenario faced by many companies is that even when they've made significant improvements to many of their attraction processes for some positions, they still struggle to find good people. It's a dead end. They simply can't fill their vacancies. The recruiter gives up and the organisation is forced to adjust its business objectives—like the global retailing CEO who told me he'd put all his expansion plans on hold because his company was simply unable to get and keep good staff.

Good applicants come in all shapes and sizes

As Confucius says, the problem is not the goals, but the action steps used to reach them. There is a way forward from this point.

In the examples I gave at the beginning of this chapter, the Marriott Hotel, St George Bank and the bus company changed their attractors to entice more candidates to apply. Yet often the reason why organisations can't attract good candidates is that their conventional target market is too limited—that is, the type of people they're looking for is too small or non-existent. As well as changing their attractors then, organisations may also need to modify their thinking as to who are the most suitable applicants to fill their vacancies.

For instance, when the Four Seasons group opened a deluxe hotel in Hawaii, they found it difficult to find trained staff to fill their vacancies and often employed people from the mainland. These imported workers tended not to stay very long, which led to high staff turnover and poor client servicing. Over time, the company realised that they had completely overlooked a large candidate pool that could fill all their positions: hardworking people employed on the local pineapple farms. They began to target these great-attitude workers, trained them in the necessary skills and became the number-one hotel on the island within 12 months.

Or take the fibre-glassing supervisor who realised that females, with their smaller hands, were perfect recruits for the new resin infusion technique that had just been developed. We filled all his vacancies with women and had no competition as other businesses had never even thought about this possibility. The Australian Defence Force had a similar experience. They made the decision to allow mild asthmatics to join up and increased their potential recruiting pool by 400 000, after years of banning asthmatics. And I'm sure those New York law firms who are renowned for competing only for Harvard, Stanford and Yale highflying graduates would find some spectacular top talent at other colleges around the country.

Considering other candidate pools takes hiring out of a small box, opens up a whole new world of applicants (see figure 3.3) and gives a company a real competitive edge. While other businesses are still vying for conventional recruits, an organisation can fill all its positions with applicants its rivals have never even considered. Even better, because these people have been given a new and unlooked-for opportunity in their lives they tend to be grateful, positive, loyal and committed to excellence to justify this uncommon belief in them.

Figure 3.3: identifying other candidate pools

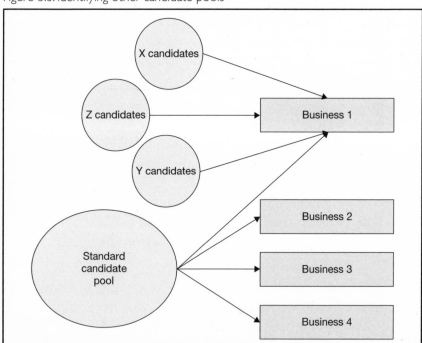

Here are some examples of demographics that organisations can target.

- *School and college graduates.* Graduates can fill entry-level positions and be trained in the skills required. For instance, the auditing firm PricewaterhouseCoopers announced in late 2007 that they were head-hunting high-performing 16-year-old school children because they could no longer fill their accountancy vacancies with university graduates. The ADF introduced a 'gap year' program, during which school leavers can come and work for them, in the hope that many will stay on. With a multitude of exciting roles to choose from, a 40 000-dollar salary and only one year's commitment, this has proved a compelling proposition for many school leavers.

- *Other gender or ethnic groups.* Many organisations have restrictive rules that preclude some candidates. When the Victorian state police changed their fitness test from six minutes to six and a half minutes, they increased their female recruits from 26 per cent to 41 per cent. Similarly, an English-language requirement may be imperative for face-to-face positions but it's not necessary for many manual jobs. In these jobs a good attitude to work is the primary need.

- *Mature workers.* As baby boomers age, this group is growing. In the past, when wages were based on experience, older workers became more expensive to hire as they aged. Many older people are now more interested in flexible work hours and whether the role/company is a good fit with their personal values. The Australian state of Victoria has just bolstered police ranks by employing retired officers to work part-time on Thursday, Friday and Saturday nights. Home Depot in the US did a deal with the AARP—an 'over 50' association with 36 million members—and now sources most of the staff for its new shops from this pool.

- *Overseas applicants.* Ten years ago I would never have considered this an option. Increasing skills shortages now make overseas applicants a growing necessity. I've sourced engineers from the UK and cabinetmakers from New Zealand. At the time, the cost of living in Australia was favourable and wages were higher so it was an attractive proposition for them. There are now a number of companies that facilitate this overseas recruitment process.

- *Boomerangs.* Employees who have left an organisation and then return make great recruits because they already have knowledge of and share the corporation's vision and values. The key to this is not to burn bridges at the time they exit. Have an open-door policy so that good people who leave know they can come back whenever suits them. Professional service firm Deloittes Touche Tohmatsu recruits as many as one-third of all its new hires from boomerangs and saves the company millions of dollars in hiring and training costs.

- *People already within the company.* I love this category because it provides learning, variety and brightness of future for everyone within a corporation. There's often someone within an organisation who can be trained into a position you're trying to fill. One of my most successful recruits was Brian, a 19-year-old I employed as a CAD draftsperson after transferring him from his previous position in the IT department. He had no CAD skills but was positive, an excellent communicator and offered to share the cost of the course to bring him up to speed on the desired technology. We decided to give him a go. Not only was he fully qualified in CAD skills within six months but he eventually became one of the company's most successful project managers because of his great attitude and interpersonal abilities.

- *Outsourcing.* From 2000 to 2010 organisations spent about five hundred million US dollars in outsourcing and McKinsey experts anticipate that by 2020 organisations will be averaging US$500 million per year—a tenfold increase. Outsourcing is good for project work and for businesses that don't have critical mass to bring specialised services in-house because they can get experienced part-time consultants who can make more impact with their practical knowledge and expertise than a less experienced full-timer on the same wage. There are some real down sides, however, as outsourced contractors are prone to little emotional attachment to an organisation and research has shown that this can lead to negative behaviour and limited employee engagement. It's fairly evident that many outsourced companies' goals are based only on their own project income, not client results, and this can also cause problems. Perhaps this is the reason why many large organisations that were fervent advocates of outsourcing 10 years ago have now brought many services back in-house.

- *Role-splitting.* In a tight labour market an organisation needs to ask itself whether it really needs to employ a person for a particular position. For hard-to-fill roles there are often parts of the job that can be performed by other recruits. In the US, a lack of teaching staff prompted the development of a lesser skilled Teacher's Assistant position, which took on all the administration and reduced the number of qualified teachers required.

The attraction cycle

By placing an applicant and their needs at the crux of the system, as shown in figure 3.4 (overleaf), organisations create a cycle of continuous improvement.

As well as attracting more good recruits, this has an added benefit. The new people-centred business practices also inspire existing employees to become more engaged and motivated, which leads to lower staff turnover and improved business results. Hence this process is a key step in building organisational excellence as well.

Figure 3.4 demonstrates that the traditional tool used by most organisations—the job ad—is only one factor in the greater whole. By taking the time to think about what people want before spending thousands on recruitment ads, not only can companies fill all their vacancies, they can also target recruits specifically suited to their business practices. As best-selling author Jim Collins points out in his book *Good to Great*, 'People are not your most important asset. The *right* people are'. This begins with attraction.

Figure 3.4: the attraction cycle

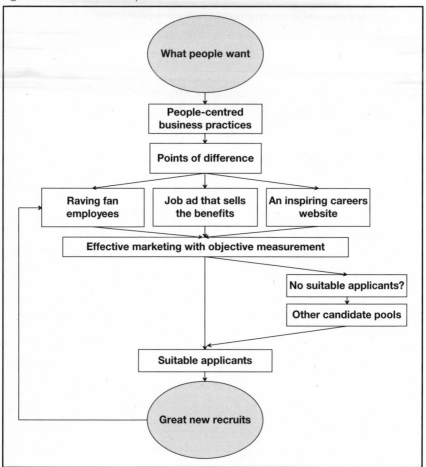

Attracting great people

Answer the following questions to assess how your organisation can attract great recruits.

→ How can we attract more candidates to our organisation in terms of:

- o time?

- o brightness of future?

- o engaging job roles?

- o inspiring them?

→ What are our organisation's points of difference when it comes to hiring?

→ What business practices can we change to create more compelling attractors?

→ Are our employees currently raving fans? If not, what do we have to change to make them raving fans?

→ Do we have a careers website? If so, does it inspire prospective candidates and sell the objective benefits of working for the company?

→ Do our job ads:

- o sell the benefits at the top?

- o consist of specific, objective facts?

- o have an indicative salary?

- o use the company logo?

→ Do we have a standard, well-thought-out ad template that sells the organisation and can be used for any job?

→ Do we have an objective measuring system in place to gauge the success of our recruitment marketing?

→ What other candidate pools could we consider using to fill our difficult vacancies?

CHAPTER 4

Screening: using objective tools to measure attitude, skills and practical fit

Brain: an apparatus with which we think we think.

Ambrose Bierce, US author and satirist

Some years ago my workload was overwhelming so I employed someone to vet résumés and do all my recruitment administration. I still conducted the interviews so I could make sure we hired the right recruits. A few months later the new HR person was struggling to find any good candidates, our managers were screaming at us because we couldn't fill their vacancies and our staff turnover had shot to an alarming 45 per cent as the new people we employed left in droves.

This didn't make sense to me. We had an effective recruitment ad, the labour market hadn't changed in any significant way and I was still using my normal methods of interviewing. It wasn't until I went back through the CVs from the previous three months that I discovered the real culprit: we'd been screening out all the good candidates.

This made me realise that one of the biggest untruths in recruitment is, 'We pretty much know the sorts of candidates we're looking for'. In my experience, most employers *think* they do, but they don't—and the reason why is obvious. People are complex, diverse and contradictory animals. Appearances are deceiving, which is why first impressions are so often wrong. Recruiters reviewing CVs have to make snap decisions about people from reading just a few flimsy pages. The surprise isn't that many organisations are poor at screening, but that any get it right at all!

In my case, my new HR person had knocked back most of the applicants that I would have considered suitable, so I'd been interviewing people who were normally my rejects and employing the best of this bad bunch. Because I hadn't been monitoring the screening process, I hadn't realised this was happening, which meant that despite our outstanding ads and effective interview system, we were no better off than the poorest recruiter. Figure 4.1 gives a comparison of effective and ineffective CV screening processes.

Figure 4.1: comparison between ineffective and effective CV screening processes

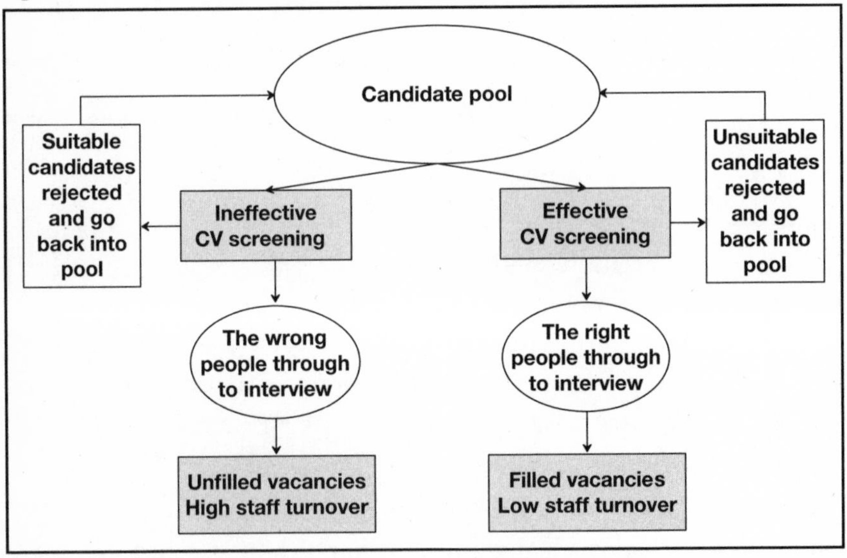

This was my fault. I'd brain-dumped my screening approach to my HR helper but, without a tangible system to back it up, she'd reverted to subjective vetting using her own 'gut feel'. If I wanted her to screen CVs with the ruthlessly efficient system that I had in my head, I had to start from scratch. I had to develop a universal, step-by-step guide that she could use to assess all candidates for any role to achieve consistent recruitment success. I had to systemise my 'gut feel' and only then could I step away and give my attention to other areas of the operation.

The best predictor of future behaviour

It sounded simple, but in practice it proved challenging. CVs are intentionally misleading documents as they're designed to accentuate strengths and ignore deficiencies. The outsourcing to so-called 'professional' CV writing companies has added to the murk. There's now a mass market of generic résumés full of 'junk' statements in which people subjectively claim something unprovable about themselves, such as:

- 'I'm a team player'

- 'I'm a good communicator'

- 'My strength is my attention to detail' (I'm often amused by the many CVs I receive by email with this statement listed as a key strength while the attachment is riddled with spelling errors).

With these types of statements, the candidate tells the employer what they want to hear. Unfortunately, another great truth of recruitment is that what people say about themselves and the reality are often poles apart. Saying 'I'm a brilliant, witty conversationalist with an IQ off the scale' doesn't make me one.

When scanning CVs, I always ignore these junk statements and look beyond them to the objective facts. For example, if someone has worked in a call centre for the past four years and has a good reference from their employer, there's a high probability that they're a team player. If they've been hands-on managing a team of 25 people with demonstrated success in their business goals, chances are they're a good communicator. However, if they've worked for three different companies in the past 18 months, my alarm bells clang: they're almost certainly a high-risk recruit.

These examples show that the only way to effectively screen CVs is to look at existing evidence of a person's working background. Words are worse than useless. Actions are everything. I have a recruitment mantra for screening that's integral to my system:

Past performance is the best predictor of future behaviour.

Everything else is just hearsay.

The core ingredients of past performance

So I had to articulate which aspects of past performance were important to me. From reading thousands of CVs and tracking the results over many years, I'd worked out that the most effective attributes I could use to define what I wanted as screening criteria, and that would give me recruitment success, were:

- attitude
- skills and qualifications
- practical fit.

These, of course, are not news. They're often mentioned in HR books and even my HR helper told me these were the categories she'd been using to review CVs. The trick, however, lies in the 'how'. Like most recruiters, my assistant had a tangible method for reviewing skills and qualifications, but when it came to attitude and practical fit, even though she *thought* she knew how to screen for them, it was really just 'gut feel'.

For example, when I asked her how she was screening for attitude, she explained that she looked for 'enthusiasm' in the cover letter. As I had learned from my very first hiring failure—a consultant who only lasted a week—there's no statistical correlation between enthusiasm and longevity. It's also impossible to measure in objective terms—say on a scale of 1 to 10—especially if the résumé is written by a professional CV company.

This is where the system had fallen down, and it's a challenge many employers have. I realised this was my real point of difference. Even though I'd never articulated them before, I only ever used *objective* criteria for screening CVs. This was a key factor in my hiring system and if my recruitment successor was ever going to be able to replicate my success, I needed to document them one by one. So I did just that, and here they are.

Screening for attitude

Attitude screening is not straightforward, so it took me a number of years of trials and testing to work out that the key objective evidence to use when vetting for attitude in CVs is:

- job stability and early workforce participation
- a pattern of completion
- a pattern of demonstrated achievement
- community involvement (as an adjunct—not relevant on its own)
- speed of application
- commitment in cover email/letter and targeted CV.

In chapter 1 I talked about the top five attitudes shared by my most successful recruits. Here's how the criteria above can be applied to each of those five attitudes when screening CVs for the recruits with the best attitude.

1 Positive work ethic

The most useful objective indicator for a positive work ethic is job stability. Someone having been in the workplace for 10 years but having a different employer every single year indicates a poor work ethic. It may be that they find it difficult to deal with authority figures, are argumentative with their workmates, or maybe they simply lack commitment or perseverance when the going gets tough. It doesn't matter what the reason is. All that matters is that they're statistically unlikely to stay more than 12 months in any organisation. I had a 95 per cent turnover of all recruits in this category, to the point that I now place them straight on the 'no' pile when screening, *regardless of their skill levels.*

Early participation in the workforce can also be a helpful indicator. Most of my best recruits had worked from a young age. They may have had a job during secondary school, worked in their parents' small business on weekends or been raised on a farm where doing chores was the norm. Whatever the case, they were used to applying themselves and reaping a reward for their hard work.

2 Perseverance

To analyse people's past performance in relation to perseverance, I look at their completion history and tally up a score as I read through the CV. Did they complete secondary school? Yes: one point on the positive side. Did they drop out before finishing their university degree? Uh oh: a point to the negative. Do they have any long, unexplained gaps in their CV? Another minus. Have they stayed with companies for 18 months or longer? Yes: this is a plus. Have they completed things in their personal life such as attaining a judo belt or reaching a high piano grade? Yes: more positive points. By the time I finish reading the CV, I have a tally. The ideal recruit is someone with all pluses and no minuses. Those who have a lot more positives than negatives (say, 7 versus 2) are also okay. Anyone with more negatives than positives is a definite 'no' and I put their CV straight on the rejection pile.

You can see from this that patterns are the most important element when it comes to measuring attitude, which is why the strict rejection policy some companies have for one-off 'failures' or the answer to one specific question can really impact on their hiring success. It doesn't matter if someone dropped out of a degree if they have demonstrated perseverance in other aspects of their life. For all you know the course may have been the wrong career choice for them, and quitting was a necessary step. But if the applicant dropped out of college and has moved from job to job every year for the past 15 years, it shows a real pattern that when the going gets tough, they move on.

The reverse is also true. Many people may show little evidence of achievement in their early lives, but examples of their perseverance begin to show up over time. For instance, some of my best candidates were those who completed a university degree later in life. This demonstrates enormous determination as they often have to persevere through several years of financial hardship, while holding down a full-time job, to achieve their dreams. They then usually apply this same level of resolve to any challenges they may face within an organisation.

3 Demonstrated achievement

This factor is perhaps the easiest one to gauge from a CV. You're looking here for a history of past achievements, which can include such things as:

- general or sporting awards/prizes in early life—for example, 'Under 12s rugby champion'

- positions of responsibility at school—for example, school prefect or house leader

- educational achievements at school and university

- awards/prizes at work—for example, top salesperson in March

- promotion/position of responsibility at work—for example, to assistant manager, manager or mentor

- stand-out workplace achievements such as managing a business or team that doubled profit in one year.

There are a couple of important points to note here. The achievements are only relevant if they're objective. For instance, a prize for 'Most Popular' or 'Friendliest Employee' means very little. Also be wary of collaborative efforts. Someone may have been a part of the 'Most Profitable Team', but you may find their only contribution was that they joined the team two weeks before the prize was awarded. 'Most Profitable Salesperson', however, is a whole different ball game.

Similarly, general or sporting awards by themselves are not indicative without a follow-on history of achievement. It's the pattern that's important. If the sporting award is backed up with other achievements, such as a promotion at work, then it's useful as a measurement.

Finally, be warned that there are applicants—I call them 'corporate parasites'—who have CVs full of artificial achievement. They have a certain level of ability and/or charisma, which has enabled them to reach manager status, but they're only interested in feathering their own nest, not furthering the aims of any company. They're difficult to detect because they choose executive roles in large organisations with little individual accountability. This also gives them achievements on paper such as 'managing 10 teams of 50 people each and achieving budgeted figures'. Once again, workplace stability is an important indicator here as workers of this type aren't interested in growing anything, so they have a history of moving on every 18 months to two years, just before their shortcomings become apparent. Referees are often lukewarm about them as well.

4 Demonstrated ability to work with people without conflict

The best way to identify a poor attitude here is through an unstable work history because when applicants repeatedly conflict with co-workers and managers they have to change jobs frequently. This is an attitude that's easy to pick up at the interview stage as people often reveal their negativity towards colleagues in their pattern of answers to interview questions.

Community or charity involvement, participation in work projects or mentoring can also be positive evidence here, though by itself it's not an indicator of a great recruit. It's only in conjunction with demonstrated achievement that it's relevant. Otherwise the candidate may be what I call the workplace 'coffee-maker'—the person who's always running around doing things for other people to compensate for a lack of achievement in their actual job role.

5 Commitment to the job role and company

There are some excellent pointers for a person's commitment. For a start, if a person is genuinely interested, they'll send their CV in quickly, so speed of application is indicative. As detailed in chapter 1, my best recruits almost always applied in the first five days after the ad was placed.

Committed candidates will also want to sell their benefits to the company so they usually send in a personalised cover letter/email, not just one sentence saying, 'Please find my CV attached, Yours sincerely …' If most of their cover letter/email addresses the selection criteria and really sells their personal benefits, this also demonstrates that they're a committed applicant. For example, 'You asked for someone with prior sales experience. I have worked for Jones Hi-Fi for four years and I won their top sales award the past two years in a row'.

If they focus on what the job will do for them, rather than the other way around, this is the sign of a poor candidate. An example would be, 'I was very excited when I saw this job advertised. I've always wanted to work in the music industry and the interstate travel would be a fabulous way for me to see more of America'.

Demonstrating company knowledge in their cover letter/email is also an indicator that it's not just a mass send-out. Many of the new, automated job application sites don't ask for a cover email, which I find astounding as it means they omit all this useful evidence. In these cases, apart from speed, the only way to ascertain commitment is to observe whether the applicant has emphasised through the content of their CV how they meet the selection criteria, and this is only useful if the sender hasn't targeted it for the job role. For example, if a business is recruiting for a sales position and the applicant has been a CAD designer for 25 years and doesn't mention sales at all in their CV, then they're not serious about the position.

If I'm not sure of the level of commitment from reading the CV, I make a quick phone call to the candidate. Those who aren't serious often respond to my introduction with, 'Who did you say you are? Where are you from? I'm sorry, I've sent so many applications out that I can't quite remember which job was yours …' With the advent of internet job-search sites, mass CV send-outs are endemic, so this is now quite a common occurrence.

I also judge candidates on the professional presentation of their CV. Those who have taken little time or effort with it demonstrate to me that they're not committed to my advertised position. This is dependent on the job role, however. I don't care if blue-collar workers don't have a formal CV if written presentation is not relevant to their work. I simply ask them to write down their job history and achievements on a piece of paper and email, deliver or post it to me, which simplifies their application process and ensures I don't alienate my most suitable recruits.

When to screen for attitude

Figure 4.2 gives a summary of the screening criteria that apply to each of the five attitudes.

Figure 4.2: summary of useful screening criteria for each attitude

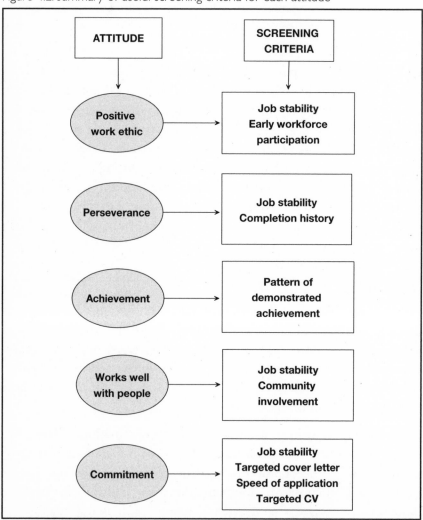

It's important to screen for all of these, no matter what job role is being filled. Whether the position is for a babysitter, a bar attendant, an IT manager or a CEO, these attitudes are crucial to a candidate's success in the role. (The only exception is achievement, which—as I explained in chapter 1—is unnecessary if the role does not require further growth.)

Take job stability, a factor in four of the five attitudes. Employers often don't want to believe this is important for all roles. When recruiting for a large cycling company that was desperate for mechanics, against my advice the CEO employed three people who were highly skilled but had demonstrated little past job stability. All were a disaster. Two turned over within three months and the other one repeatedly conflicted with staff and clients, was a performance management nightmare and was eventually sacked.

Another client told me that because her new employee was only a short-term contractor she 'didn't worry about that job stability stuff'. Two months later, when he was difficult to manage, not delivering and her project had run well over time, she reconsidered her stance.

I've been guilty of this myself. I employed a bookkeeper, to come in once a quarter to keep my home accounts up-to-date. Because I was very busy at work at the time, I employed a person who was advertising in my local paper without doing my usual job stability check. The next few months were hell. The bookkeeper was negative, confrontational and made constant errors. I was fortunate that she quit to take up a full-time job before I had to sack her. I learned a valuable lesson though: attitudes are important no matter how minimal the role. For my next bookkeeper, I took my time and did stringent screening. She has now been working for me, without issue, for five years.

I cannot emphasise this enough. There is *always* a reason why some people turn over jobs on a regular basis, and they will always be very high-risk recruits, no matter what their skills. The only exceptions to this rule are young applicants less than five years out of school or university. For these candidates, a certain amount of job turnover is natural as they experiment with careers to find one that suits. In these cases, evidence such as early workforce participation, and patterns of demonstrated achievement and completion are more important factors for determining attitude than is job stability.

People often ask me whether Generation Y, characterised by the media and various HR experts as 'low commitment', should be screened differently from other applicants. The answer is 'no'. I don't buy into the myth that all Generation Ys are uncommitted the same way that I don't believe that all Baby Boomers are selfish. Sure, I've read many reports saying they're demanding and that they want more attention and more perks at work, but I believe what they want is world-class people practices. It's just that in the new twenty-first-century recruitment paradigm the vast majority of 'less than great' companies have not caught up, don't provide these, and when young people leave, blame the lazy, distracted Ys for their own failures.

Screening for skills and qualifications

I've emphasised attitude as a key factor in hiring, but you obviously can't ignore skills and qualifications. A teacher needs a formal teaching qualification; a doctor a medical degree; and a truck driver is useless without a heavy vehicle licence. As these are always included in a CV, this is the most straightforward screening area.

As well as the actual qualifications, I also look at quality. Was the tertiary degree from a top university or a mediocre one? Did the person achieve a high rating or do an honours course? Does the training establishment have a good reputation or does it churn out thousands of second-rate apprentices each year? Is the certificate authentic? (This is becoming more important these days with fake certificates available for purchase over the internet.)

When I first started hiring in the UK, I wasn't familiar with the reputation of each institution so I researched them and also tracked all my best recruits to work out where they came from. The statistical correlation was striking. I also discovered that the volume of training was irrelevant to a candidate's success. Many people include every workshop they've ever attended on their CV, even those that are unrelated to the advertised position. Attendance is not achievement, however. If someone had to be in the top 10 per cent of their class to get a place in a course, that's relevant. If not, it's just more junk to pad out a CV.

Screening for practical fit

As well as skills and attitudes, there's one last factor to take into account when it comes to identifying the right person for a role and an organisation. That factor is practical fit: the specific factors about a company or position that, if matched with a candidate, lower the statistical risk of turnover.

Recruiting without practical fit is like trying to force a square peg into a round hole. The applicant may have the skills and attitudes that an organisation wants, but if what they're looking for doesn't align with the job role or the organisation, they're guaranteed to turn over.

This often involves some re-jigging. I did some recruitment for a rural resort that had constant turnover of hotel managers. When I analysed why, I realised that the recruitment advertising was attracting highfliers all right, but they were all city-based executives who had failed to adapt to the remote environment. We changed the ad and made the country life a selling point. The next manager was a well-qualified hotel executive who had grown up in a country town and wanted to raise his children in one. It was a good fit for him and a good fit for the hotel.

Criteria for practical fit are dependent on the job role and the corporation, but here are a few general ones to consider.

Organisational culture

Most organisations have some ingrained cultural values and practices that are integral to their success. Being aware of these kinds of cultural requirements *before* even starting to screen is another key to hiring success. No matter how skilled an applicant, a bad fit here leads to poor results and constant staff turnover.

Someone who has worked in only incentivised, sales-based roles, for example, may find it difficult working on a flat wage. Employees with a government background often struggle to make the switch to private enterprise, and vice versa. Military leaders may not be suited to less authoritarian establishments. Someone who has worked for a large organisation may find it an effort working within the limited resources of a small start-up business. Whatever the requirement, the closer the match, the better the recruitment outcome.

Position-specific requirements

There are often specific requirements for a position that need to be matched with an applicant.

- *Salary package.* If a candidate is currently earning much more than the role on offer and they don't offer an explanation for this mismatch, such as, 'I'm attracted by the flexible work hours', they're usually unsuitable for the position. Recruiters often tell me, 'I had the perfect person for the position but they wanted a higher salary'. This means they weren't the perfect person. If they were, they would see and enthuse about the benefits of the position themselves as it would align with all their personal requirements. A mismatch in salary means the recruiter is not targeting the best-fit people for the position.

- *Geography.* Local candidates are always the best fit for a position. This is because they have already demonstrated that they like living somewhere. Those who relocate are higher risk because they often find that they, or their partner or their children, hate the area, or that it's too stressful finding new schools, doctors, banks and other contacts away from their established family and friends network. There's also extra cost and time involved in relocation as the new recruit will need more general support for the first few months to get set up. There are, of course, always those who thrive on change, and these people will have a demonstrated history of moving, travelling and/or adapting to differing circumstances.

Geographical fit can also apply to commuters. I've had almost 100 per cent turnover of recruits who had to travel long hours to work every day, regardless of the calibre of their application or their stated commitment to the position. No matter how good a fit someone is in attitude and skill, if their work–life balance is poor they will eventually look for another option.

- *Hours.* The hours worked and their flexibility need to match the applicant's lifestyle. If the position requires someone to dedicate themselves to 80 hours per week and the applicant has been working in a part-time job averaging 20 hours per week for the past 10 years, this is likely to result in a bad fit.

- *Team versus stand-alone position.* If an organisation is looking to fill a stand-alone position, then the best-fit applicant is one who has a track record of working solo. A great travelling salesperson who requires self-motivation and discipline is unlikely to be someone who has worked as part of a manager-led team for 10 years.

The candidate-screening checklist

Once I'd identified the above factors as the key evidence for vetting CVs, I was able to develop a standard, universal screening system. I gave this to my HR helper and my organisation's recruitment success skyrocketed. I now had the mechanism to train more people in effective screening techniques and ensure consistent, objective hiring throughout the company.

I created a practical tool: a simple checklist that assessed attitude, skills and practical fit and acted as a first filter (see my screening checklist in table 4.1, overleaf). Creating a document like this for each job role forces an organisation to think carefully about the *objective* selection criteria before advertising the position. This leads to a better decision-making process and reduces conflict between multiple recruiters as everyone agrees on the desired outcomes in advance.

Table 4.1: CV screening checklist for objective and comprehensive candidate assessment

Name:
Vacancy:

Attitutue	Poor	Average	Good	Overall	Phone?	Interview?
Positive work ethic (job stability/early jobs)						
Perseverance (completion history)						
Achievement (past achievements)						
No conflict (job stability/community involvement)						
Commitment (speed/targeted application)						
Skills	No	Some	Yes			
Sales experience						
Sales potential						
Customer service experience						
Practical fit	Poor	Average	Good			
Location (close to store)						
Demonstrated shift flexibility in past roles						
Salary match (similar in past roles)						
Cultural fit (worked in similar retail environment)						
Personal presentation (CV and cover email)						
Availability						
Other criteria	No	Yes				
Meets visa requirements	A 'no' on visa is an instant fail					
Applicable second language						
Education						

General comments

This checklist also allowed me to assess candidates more objectively. First I scored each candidate on attitude. I rejected those who scored 'Poor' on any of the five factors straight away. I then rated the rest on skills and practical fit as well. Applicants who scored well in all areas were instant standouts. Those who rated well in most aspects also passed through to the next screening stage, albeit with comments about areas that needed questioning in order to better understand the applicants. Poor candidates who had failed to meet these other criteria were rejected at this point.

As 'Skills' was only one of the three factors in this assessment (the other two being attitude and practical fit), the number of applicants who made it through to the next screening stage was considerably fewer than those who would get through on just the skills check (which is the norm for many organisations). This more comprehensive vetting also meant that candidates successful through to interview were a much better fit with the role and organisation.

Making contact

The next step in the screening process was to contact all the candidates who had scored well in the checklist. This quick phone or Skype call saves a lot of time because it allows the recruiter to further whittle down the number of applicants so that only those who are suitable for the position end up at interview. I'm always shocked when, for example, I see someone proudly conducting 30 face-to-face interviews for a fork-lift driver because their screening is based only on whether the applicant has a forklift licence. This time could be far better spent identifying the best candidates or improving recruitment systems.

My system for phone screening is very simple. I introduce myself in a warm and friendly manner, ask the caller if they have time to speak now and then say I'm processing all the CVs for the role and have a couple of questions in regard to their application. I then ask for clarification on grey areas I've previously identified, such as why they're applying for an 80-hour-a-week position when they've always worked part-time in the past.

I also use this call to gather more concrete evidence. If a person is very long-winded and they're applying for a call-centre position where speed and succinctness are vital, then they're not a good practical fit. If they speak negatively about every person they work with, or externalise all their problems, then they fail my attitude test. If they show little interest in the job role or organisation, then I know they're not committed.

When a candidate has been a standout on my checklist, with no areas needing clarification, I use the call as a sales opportunity to create a positive first impression. I ask a couple of general questions such as, 'You've been working at Jones Electrics for four years now. Why are you looking to leave? What was it about this job that attracted you?'

If their answer matches what I'm offering and they demonstrate they've really thought about it, I can then sell the benefits of the job in more detail and get them excited about the role. I can also find out what other job interviews they have in the pipeline so I can diarise to book mine in at an earlier date.

Most employers miss this sales aspect of phone screening. As the first point of human contact in hiring, it's a vital step in the process. Often these calls are palmed off to HR administrators, who fail to inspire with their production line approach and repel suitable candidates *before* they even reach the interview stage.

I always finish the call by thanking the candidate for their time and advising them that I'll let them know if they've been successful through to interview. Those who are suitable, I then call the following morning to book in a time as soon as possible. Speed, speed and more speed!

Tracking great candidate attributes — the data-driven approach

Once I began applying my new CV screening system, I discovered another big advantage. I found I could use them to track my most successful candidates over time, work out the evidence that gave me the best retention rates for different positions and then create checklists based around these attributes. This is very useful, especially in large organisations that recruit many people in the same roles.

For example, when recruiting for travel agents I found I had a 95 per cent success rate when I employed applicants with these five criteria:

1 A tertiary degree.

2 Excellent communication skills.

3 Travel to at least two continents.

4 Past achievement in any field.

5 A stable job history—that is, someone who had not changed jobs every 12 months.

Those without a tertiary degree or demonstrated past achievement dropped to a retention rate of 45 per cent. Those with a patchy work history had a 5 per cent retention rate. Note that I'm not saying here that a person without a tertiary degree would not make a successful travel consultant. Fifty-five per cent of them do. This is just about statistical risk. The less risk an organisation takes, the lower its staff turnover. When I couldn't source applicants who ticked all five criteria, I employed applicants without tertiary degrees but only ones with good, stable work histories and a lot of demonstrated achievement. In that way, I kept my risk to a minimum.

Google, who topped the Fortune 500 'Best Employer' List in 2012 and 2013, is also using this kind of data-driven approach. By analysing information from existing highfliers, they created an effective hiring algorithm that predicted which of their new applicants had the highest probability of succeeding. They also calculated that a highflier was an astonishing 300 times better in terms of performance results than an average employee.

Most organisations don't have Google's IT power, but as I found when measuring attributes, it is possible to do a lot of data analysis manually using checklists and spreadsheets. Be wary of pseudo-science, however. Often when I ask organisations to identify the characteristics of their most suitable candidates, they come up with competencies such as 'creative skill' or 'good change management' and many have built these traits into complex hiring systems. Yet even though this strategy appears scientific, without any objective method to measure this kind of nebulous criteria it has about the same success rate as the old 'gut instinct' interview.

The whole screening cycle

You can see that the screening cycle begins with the employer identifying what they want—that is, their desired attributes for the right candidate (compared with attraction, where the focus is on what the candidate wants). This process usually occurs before advertising to allow for targeted marketing. By identifying the attitude, skills and practical fit necessary for each job role—and tracking these selection criteria—effective screening becomes a cyclical process of continuous improvement, as you can see in figure 4.3.

Figure 4.3: the screening process

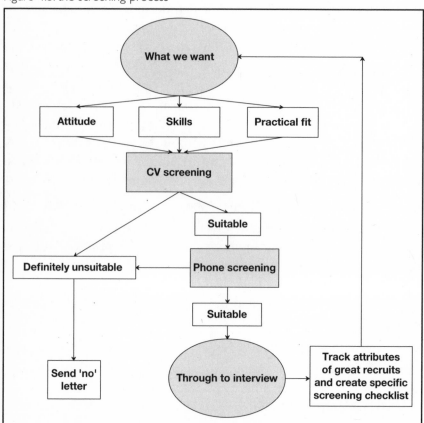

This also makes it easier for organisations to adapt to change in the labour market because criteria can be altered to reflect other candidate pools when skills shortages kick in.

Other screening tools and resources

The advent of online job-search sites and the ability for candidates to send hundreds of CVs out at just the push of a button have together created extra challenges for most employers. Finding the one or two suitable candidates among the thousands who apply is like panning for gold in a muddy river. A simple non-invasive method of winnowing is to build five to 10 essential skills and practical-fit questions into the initial application process. Asking if someone has a heavy vehicle licence or a residency visa won't annoy applicants, but it will filter out those who are blatantly unsuitable. Using attitudinal questions here won't work, though, because without a context they will definitely screen out good people.

These questions can be part of a manual document, but if they're automated they cut down a lot of work. For smaller businesses that can't afford their own IT programs, there are recruitment marketing businesses that, for a small fee, let you use their candidate management systems and allow you to custom build these kinds of application questions. The time saved in vetting a much smaller percentage of CVs will far outweigh this initial investment.

Hundreds of other service companies have now also sprung up that help employers with their initial screening. Here are my thoughts on some of the main types.

Automated phone filters

Often large organisations conducting mass ongoing employment drives use an automated phone system as a basic first filter for screening criteria, especially for lower-level roles. Applicants ring up, answer a few questions and their answers are used to determine whether they are suitable. They are then invited to send in their CV. Those who are deemed unsuitable are knocked out straight away, saving the organisation time and energy in screening hundreds of applications.

It all sounds good in theory. The problem is in the delivery. My friend Janine applied to a company that had outsourced this process overseas. Not only was the phone line quality poor, but the unfamiliar accent of the automated examiner made it impossible for her to understand the questions. After her third try she rang the company to ask for help, and was told by a friendly receptionist that their policy was only to communicate with applicants successful through the initial phone screening. Janine now works for someone else.

The follow-through of organisations that use these systems can also be inadequate. My niece Courtney and six of her school friends—all achievers—applied for the same job at different times over a 12-month period with a large global fast-food retailer using this system. The response, three months after application, was an email to all the individuals saying, 'Thank you for coming along to our interview' (which they hadn't). 'You have been unsuccessful'. The girls now refuse to eat at this burger chain, which demonstrates the negative effect of poor recruitment on branding and the business.

This kind of experience definitely fails my 'make a positive first impression' rule. I'm not against these phone filters in principle. I just haven't seen one that works.

Recruitment agencies

Recruitment agencies are useful if an organisation needs to increase its candidate pool or has no expertise in-house. As an initial screening mechanism, however, they suffer from the same handicap as the rest of the industry in that many use only subjective opinion when it comes to screening for attitude. This is demonstrated in many candidate market reports, which are often simply a summary of what the person said in the interview, such as:

- 'Belinda said she was a team player and she enjoys working with people.'
- 'Joe lists his strengths as communication and attention to detail.'
- 'Penelope would like a role where she is challenged and can reach her potential.'

As I've already pointed out, these kinds of statements, without objective evidence to back them up, are meaningless to an employer. I always use agencies when I need to expand my candidate pool, but I ask for the CVs, rather than relying on market reports, and then screen them myself using my standard attitude criteria.

Some employers use recruitment agencies because they're too busy to run the hiring process themselves, which is ironic because:

Recruitment agencies don't save you time.

Using an effective agency can have a lot of benefits, but selecting the right agency, building a relationship and managing them is a lengthy process. Because of the nature of recruitment as a discipline, there are hundreds of agencies, but no standard recognised hiring system. I've worked with some delightful agencies that made a big effort to supply me with applicants to suit my needs. I've also dealt with others who do minimal screening and then blitz my email inbox with hundreds of unsuitable CVs in the vain hope that one might strike the target. It takes time, thought and commitment to research and select the agencies that best suit your organisation's needs.

Also remember that recruitment is a sales system, and using an agency means an organisation is, in essence, selling through a third party. Time-poor executives often give agency consultants only sketchy details about the available position and are then too busy to answer queries or take calls — and then they blame the recruitment consultant for the lack of hiring success. The real culprit is their own mismanagement of the process. It takes time to educate the agency in the organisation's points of difference so that they have a genuine understanding of the benefits for potential candidates.

Of course, every recruitment agency will tell you they're fabulous, so when it comes to choosing which one to work with, you need to apply an objective system—in effect, recruit the recruiter. Here are my systems for selecting and managing recruitment agencies.

Selecting

When selecting a recruitment agency, you should consider the following:

- *Past performance.* What objective evidence of hiring success can they demonstrate in regard to existing clients?

- *Skills fit.* Do they have the right candidate pool for the types of recruits you're looking for? What's their proof?

- *Recruiters.* Who are their recruiters? Do they inspire you or are they just process workers?

- *Screening effectiveness.* What's their system for screening CVs? Are they open to incorporating your requirements?

- *Sales effectiveness.* Does the agency sell itself well to clients? If so, chances are they'll be effective at selling your organisation to others.

- *Reverse recruiting.* Do they ask you as many questions as you ask them? A good agency should qualify you to make sure that the service they offer suits your needs.

Managing

By 'managing' the recruitment agency I mean you should take the time to do the following:

- *Build a good relationship.* It takes time to develop and manage a relationship with an agency, which is important when you consider that there's always competition for their best candidates.

- *Provide screening tools.* Give them a copy of your CV screening checklist and educate them in the attitudinal and practical-fit criteria that are important to you.

- *Provide selling tools.* Explain and supply your standard selling tools so that they understand and are passionate about the real benefits and points of difference of your organisation and the position being advertised.

- *Reward and recognise hiring success.* Give them positive feedback for good-fit CVs and reward them with a gift, such as a bottle of wine, for every successful candidate employed. This guarantees you'll always get first choice of the best applicants.

- *Measure effectiveness.* Measure each agency in terms of number of suitable applicants, those employed and their retention, and use this to determine repeat business. Don't use too many different agencies as this dilutes loyalty.

Also, never forget that most agencies are incentivised on placement. For the less ethical ones, this means they'll spend more time trying to sell the candidate's advantages to a client than on effective screening. My advice is to never take on a recruit who is 'iffy' simply because there's a free replacement offer. I know it's hard when you're desperate to fill a role, but it's not worth the cost in time, effort and employee morale when the new recruit inevitably turns over.

Psychometric tests as an initial screening tool

When I returned from the UK and joined Flight Centre's Australian leadership team, I was horrified to discover that the company's recruiters were making candidates sit an initial psychometric test online, and then were only passing to interview those who scored an 'A' on their chosen criteria. All other screening devices had become obsolete. There's simply no test that can give such a definitive answer on a person, so I wasn't surprised to find that the corporation was experiencing high staff turnover and low morale in a number of areas.

After I started business consulting, I found that the use of psychometric tests in this manner was increasing in popularity because of employers' growing need for a first filter. One manager told me of an administrator who had worked for him as a temp for six months and had proven to be a dedicated and efficient employee. Despite this actual evidence of past performance, when she applied for a full-time position with the company, she failed the company's initial psychometric screening test and the HR manager knocked her application on the head.

When the operations manager questioned this decision, the HR manager swore that their test was 'never wrong' in these matters but couldn't give any objective evidence to support this statement. (I could have given her some counter-evidence though, in the high staff turnover that was raging through the company at the time.) This kind of bureaucratic decision always astounds me and brings to mind Ambrose Bierce's quote:

Brain: an apparatus with which we think we think.

These tests can also impact in other ways. One of my clients was shocked to discover that they were losing 25 per cent of their best potential recruits when we began measuring the dropouts. The applicants had been asked to fill out a one-hour psychometric assessment as the first step in their hiring process, and had simply dropped out rather than taking the test. To me this is a bit like asking a potential partner to meet your parents on the first date. It's just too much commitment.

The most opportune time for assessment is *after* both parties have explored each other's suitability and formed an attachment. I've put down my thoughts on psychometric tests as a post-interview tool in chapter 6 so all I'll say here is that they're like a surgeon's scalpel. They can be helpful when used well as an adjunct to the recruitment process, but in the wrong hands—or used for the wrong purpose—they can be lethal to an organisation's hiring success, carving out suitable and unsuitable candidates alike in an indiscriminate fashion. Never, never use them as an initial screening device! The only winner will be the testing company, whose convincing marketing blurb has netted them a big profit.

Take time to save time

Using psychometric tests as a first filter is like sending in a scud missile to sort out a playground fight. You don't need to psychoanalyse candidates at this point, but just winnow out the ones that are obviously inappropriate for the role. Those organisations that use them as initial screening resources because they want to save time — or just want to be seen as applying some form of system — don't understand that taking the time to think about and identify the attributes of their best people, and using consistent objective screening tools to find them, are keys to hiring success.

They're also a major factor in retention. When my HR helper began applying my objective screening system, we didn't change anything else in our hiring process. Within three months the company had filled most of its vacancies and profits rose accordingly, and within six months staff turnover was back to acceptable levels.

I often think now about the alternative: about what would have happened if we hadn't changed what we did, if our turnover had kept increasing and our operation had continued to bleed profits. Where would the business be now? Where would I be now? As Albus Dumbledore, the wise wizard in the Harry Potter series, said, 'It is our choices Harry, that show what we truly are, far more than our abilities'.[13] When it came to screening, choosing the right people to go through to interview made all the difference.

The screening process

Use the following questions to assess how your organisation could improve its screening of recruits.

→ Do we identify objectively what we want in a candidate before advertising?

→ How can we screen candidates better in terms of:

- o attitude?

- o skills and qualifications?

- o practical fit?

→ What are our main cultural requirements for practical fit?

→ In the major roles we recruit for, what are the key screening criteria for each one?

→ Do we have a highly skilled, inspiring recruiter vetting our CVs and conducting phone screening interviews?

→ Is our application process easy to follow and implement?

→ Do we have an effective first filter system in place?

→ If we use recruitment agencies, do we:

- o select and measure them on achievement?

- o take the time to grow the relationship with them?

- o reward them for sending us great, successful candidates?

→ Do we use psychometric tests as part of our initial screening process? If so, in what way do we objectively measure them for effectiveness?

→ Is our screening process data driven?

→ Do we effectively measure our screening process?

CHAPTER 5

Interviewing: inspiring and assessing

Almost like a car salesman, if a guy walks onto the lot and a salesman qualifies him on how he is dressed he may miss out on a hell of a sale. We try to open our mind and say it's not about perception or what you think you see.

Billy Beane, General Manager of the major league Oakland A's baseball team

The book *Moneyball* (and the film based on the book), tells the story of Billy Beane, the real-life major league baseball team manager who had a dilemma. With a miniscule budget compared to most other teams he needed to identify talented, undervalued players to create a real, competitive edge, yet his existing scouts, who interviewed and appointed based on 'gut instinct', rarely seemed to pick the winners. Finally he ditched conventional wisdom, axed most of his scouts and brought in a young analyst to create objective hiring processes. By looking at the statistics of what players had actually done, rather than using traditional methods such as 'judging a player's performance simply by watching it',[14] Billy turned one of the poorest teams in American baseball into one of the most successful, and revolutionised the world of professional sports recruitment while he was at it.

The purpose of interviews

Despite Billy's obvious success, most of the other major league baseball teams haven't copied his example. For many, conventional opinions have acquired such authority of fact and these have become so entrenched in their scouting systems that they simply don't know how to start the process of re-education.

This lack of intellectual rigour in interviewing is also common in business organisations. Ironically, when I started out I was one of the biggest offenders in this area. Like many novice recruiters with no formal training, I modelled my process on my own past interviews. I talked a lot, asked questions for the sake of asking questions and didn't use any standard format at all. My methodology could be summed up as 'a contagion of bad practice'.

Then I noticed that one or two of my good candidates were dropping out after the interview. Their explanation was generally a vague, 'I didn't think the job was for me', so my assumption was that this could be put down to natural attrition. After measuring the number of dropouts, though, I was shocked to find that it was nearly 15 per cent of my A-listers.

Up to this point my belief was that the function of an interview was to screen and identify the right person for a role. After all, this is what most interview theory, practice and discussion revolves around. I now realised that the good applicants were also screening me and my organisation to determine their fit. When they left feeling unmotivated, they simply dropped out of the process before even reaching the offer stage, which demonstrates that:

A key reason people choose to work for an organisation is because the way they are interviewed inspires them.

To boost my recruitment success I had to consider:

- how to inspire interviewees
- how to assess interviewees.

Inspiring interviewees

To inspire interviewees I had to again look at some sales techniques.

Making a great first impression

According to Sales 101, it takes less than 10 seconds to make a first impression. Consider that interviewees are like new customers, assessing every factor before coming to conclusions about an organisation. Because any applicant could become 'the one'—a company's finest future employee—it's obviously in everyone's best interest to make a favourable first impression.

The invitation for an interview

This is especially important for the generations of applicants who have grown up using social media. I'm not recommending the use of jargon here ('Yo, bro, this is an awesome application!' is obviously overkill), but warm, engaging, personalised e-cards or eye-catching interview invitations make a much better impression than mass send-outs of standard, formal, depersonalised letters.

The physical office environment

A company's office space sends out a strong message to applicants and can be enhanced by decorating a waiting area with interesting plants, decor and eye-catching furniture; hanging corporate awards and pictures of employee celebrations on the walls; providing corporate brochures, marketing material or a corporate DVD for them to look at while they wait; or even just removing clutter from reception areas and interview rooms. So make it fun and interesting—not bland and sterile.

Relationship building

When I researched what applicants liked about different interviews they had attended, the 'human factor' was the statistic with the highest correlation to success. I once took a cold-calling magazine sales job with an average London company because the recruiter was such a warm and inspiring person. The reverse also applies. A friend knocked back a position paying $50 000 more than her existing salary because 'the HR person treated me like s★★t—a faceless number in an endless supply of human resources'.

It's all about paying attention to people. Compare this experience to a customer buying something big such as a house or a holiday. There's usually a single person involved in the process, answering all their questions, offering advice, and making them feel valued and appreciated. (And if they don't do this, or they get tossed around from person to person and no-one knows what's going on, they tend not to buy.) Choosing a job is a similar big decision in people's lives and that's why having a single point of contact throughout the whole process is the kind of connection that can greatly improve an organisation's chances of hiring the best recruits.

It's also why corporate attitude is so important to the interview process. Teaching people at all levels that 'we're fortunate when we employ good people', rather than the conventional, 'these hopefuls are lucky to get an interview' transforms actions and outcomes. This is especially relevant in large, bureaucratic organisations where the natural tendency is often to depersonalise processes.

Speed, speed and more speed

When I was recruiting for a night-time security officer for the yachting company, the CFO decided she wanted to be involved in the interview process, even though she would have no working contact with this employee. I finally found the perfect applicant after several weeks of searching and organised for her to meet him, but she was delayed at a meeting and cancelled with only a few hours' notice. What seemed like nothing to her was a big deal to the candidate, who had already arranged time off from work. I then rescheduled the interview for the following week. Once again, she cancelled the day before because of the more pressing, work-related activity of analysing photocopier use in relation to the purchase of paper. By this time the security guy was exasperated. I tried to keep him engaged, but I wasn't surprised when he rang to advise me he'd taken another position.

I'm all for management involvement in the interview process, but not if it's going to slow it down so much that the organisation loses its good applicants. Where it's necessary, such as for a senior or highly specialised job role, then educate everyone in the need for speed and arrange for executives to sit in on the first interview. I also do this with line managers if the position requires technical skills assessment.

In the case of the botched security guard example, the reason the CFO micro-managed all hiring decisions was because she had lumped me in with her other recruiters, who she knew were ineffective and poorly paid. This type of warped methodology is common for many organisations and intrigues me because no-one would employ a useless sales manager and then meet all the clients themselves, or hire an ineffectual marketer and then write their own advertising copy. As well as slowing the process down, micro-managing stunts recruitment innovation and expertise, which leads to even more hiring failures. There's only one solution to this: employ the right recruiter—a warm, skilled, inspiring communicator—and then give them their head.

Effective sales tools

When I first began recruiting in the UK, I had very little backup material until I received a corporate DVD from my head office in Australia. It cost my business several thousand dollars, but was well worth it as the three-minute presentation transformed the candidates' impression of the company. Even when I felt tired or demotivated, I could flick on this DVD for candidates and achieve the same inspiring result.

Standard sales tools, then, rather than recruiters' fickle and often unreliable sales skills and corporate knowledge, get the best interview results. By trialling and testing tools over time I found that the best ones were those that showcased to applicants how the role and organisational benefits contributed to their own lives (the 'What's in it for me?' factors, which are described overleaf), placing *them* at the centre of the interview process.

What's in it for me?

Sales tools that showcase to candidates what the benefits of the organisation are to them can consist of:

- *The big picture.* Show them a corporate DVD, PowerPoint presentation or display folder outlining the company vision, five-year plan and organisational points of difference, including factors such as size, location, major clients, awards, innovations, training programs, social and community programs, travel opportunities and so on.

- *Examples of actual employees' career journeys.* Demonstrate promotion from within, time taken to reach management level and/or the potential for movement across job roles or between geographical locations.

- *A summary of earning potential or a salary package guide.* Prepare a list of examples of actual wages for average and high achievers for commission-based positions, depending on the job role and the degree of negotiation involved.

- *A list of the benefits and points of difference of the actual job role.* Include comments from existing staff or podcasts of real employees talking about what they like most about the role, or run a 'Day in the Life' video or simulation.

- *A list of in-house free or discounted services.* Make this available to every employee.

- *An outline of any flexible work hours / shift times or exceptional holiday leave.* Prepare examples where the organisation offers real points of difference to its competitors.

The process of selling is as important as content. Whatever platform is used, present the facts in a fun, engaging manner, not as a list of rules and regulations that would put a policy planner to sleep.

Be careful not to oversell, though. A 2012 exit data study by Insync Surveys[15] found that 51 per cent of people leave primarily because a job doesn't satisfy them and this is often because employers, desperate to fill positions, chronically over-promise and under-deliver. When they paint too glowing a picture, and the organisation doesn't live up to the utopian ideal created in the mind of the applicant in regard to the job itself, the level of challenge or career and promotional opportunities, the new employee is guaranteed to turn over (line managers who do their own recruiting are especially guilty of this).

Supplying every recruiter in the organisation with standard, real job descriptions and genuine benefits prevents this kind of over-selling, and ensures potential employees all receive a similar message and hiring results are consistent. Here's an example:

In your first 12 months you will be overwhelmed with information and you'll be starting with no client base, so you won't make much money to begin with. If you work hard, however, you can make up to $100 000 in annual salary and, because all promotions are merit-based, you can become a manager within a year.

This type of candid approach will deter uncommitted applicants who are looking for an easy ride, and ensures that the right-fit, goal-driven people who are employed will persevere and stick around long-term.

Interview formats

The right interview format inspires applicants and contributes to recruitment success. The following is a rundown on each type.

The one-on-one interview

From the applicant's point of view, this is the most common style of interview and therefore the one with which they feel most comfortable. It's also good for the recruiter because the one-on-one attention enables them to really connect with a person by creating a favourable first impression, building up rapport, selling the benefits of the position and gaining invaluable knowledge as to what type of package to offer a successful applicant. I measured my drop-out rate for all interview types and this one had the least.

I use the term 'one-on-one'; however, this type of interview is also successful as 'two-on-one' or 'three-on-one', as long as it meets the following parameters:

- A recruiter with specialty hiring knowledge is always involved and directs the interview process.

- Others who participate are assigned a specific role in the interview — for instance, a line manager attends to ask technical questions, an executive sits in to sell the organisation to applicants for senior positions, or two specialised recruiters collaborate to overcome individual recruiter bias and set roles beforehand.

- The individuals involved recruit together on a regular basis.

The fast-track interview for boomerang employees

Employees leave for all sorts of reasons: to have babies, to travel or simply because the grass looks greener elsewhere at the time. The key is to make it easy for the good ones to come back by creating a fast-track interview system that recognises they are special and valued, and assesses their existing levels of ability and commitment.

Take my friend Maxine, an award-winning high achiever who left her company to go travelling and reapplied for a position several years later. Had any of the organisation's entrepreneurial managers known she was available they would have employed her in seconds. Unfortunately for Maxine, the HR department lobbed her in with all the new applicants and made the whole experience so excruciating that after two weeks of group interviews and bureaucratic testing to determine whether she was suitable for the job, she simply dropped out and went to work for a competing company. This is what happens in organisations without a dedicated boomerang interview system.

The group interview

The advantage of group interviewing is that it's fast (the whole process is wrapped up in one day), it's good for high-volume positions or ones you need to fill on a regular basis (such as Christmas casuals), and it's easier to make a decision as you have other applicants to use as a yardstick. The downside is that the mass interview format can be off-putting (I'd get a few no-shows every week), which is why I used to always overbook these kinds of interviews. It's also why I wouldn't recommend this interview type as suitable in tough labour markets where candidate numbers are limited, or for one-off vacancy filling.

The best way to guarantee maximum attendance is by spelling out the benefits to applicants in a phone catch-up beforehand. I always began by explaining that the group day had been designed for applicants to get a closer look at the business and find out whether it suited *their* needs; that they got to meet key executives and incumbents in the role; that they could experience actual on-the-job activities; and, if successful in the assessment process, that they would be offered a job the very next day.

Labelling the day with applicant-friendly titles such as 'New Start' or 'Career Finder', rather than an employer-centric tag such as 'Assessment Day', and making confirmation calls to participants 24 hours beforehand also goes a long way to reducing candidate apprehension and no-shows. The more personalised they are, the more successful the outcomes.

For an example of a group interview day schedule take a look at table 5.1.

Table 5.1: group interview day schedule

PART A: INSPIRATION	
Welcome Brand DVD / inspiring music playing on arrival, collect paperwork, hand out name tags Thank everyone for coming and do housekeeping such as toilet breaks / phone use	10 mins
The big picture Present DVD / PowerPoint outlining corporate story, including history, vision, long-term plan and benefits	10 mins
The role Recruiter presents information on the role, including typical activities, educational pathways, career progression opportunities, hours and benefits	25 mins

(continued)

Table 5.1: group interview day schedule *(cont'd)*

A personal story	15 mins
Recruiter or senior leader shares their story, including their journey with the company to date, career highlights, challenges overcome, and what they love about the role and the organisation. Question/Answer session at end	
'Getting-to-know-you' icebreaker	45 mins
5 mins: groups of 2 (max. 3) spend 5 mins getting to know why the other person would be great for the role	
35–40mins: each individual introduces their partner back to the group to 'sell' why they would be great for the role and the organisation	
Tea break	15 mins
PART B: ASSESSMENT	
Team activity	30 mins
Recruiters facilitate group activity and assess candidates	
5 mins: intro / explanation of activity	
15 mins: groups work through activity (5–7 people per group)	
10 mins: groups present back to recruiters	
Individual activities by rotation	30 mins
Recruiter conducts individual role play	
Candidates complete two assessment tests, including a pressure test, on rotation	
Lunch and debriefing	45 mins
Candidates are sent to lunch. Recruiters debrief and decide who is brought through to the afternoon session	
PART C: SUCCESSFUL CANDIDATE RELATIONSHIP BUILDING AND ASSESSMENT	
Congratulations!	30 mins
Congratulate successful candidates on making it through to the second stage. Recruiter runs through more detailed information, such as example salary and structures, and explains the afternoon timetable	
Candidate interviews	As required
Candidates who are successful through to the afternoon session then participate in one-on-one interview	

The best thing about group interviews is that they inspire applicants by their very design because the competitive nature of the team activities increases people's desire for the position.

The panel interview

Panel interviews differ from two-on-one or three-on-one interviews because they involve people who work in different areas of an organisation, many with no real hiring expertise, coming together to interview applicants on an irregular basis. Panel interviews are popular with some organisations, especially in the public sector, but as applicants are often just bombarded with unplanned questions, they can be uninspiring. One senior public servant I talked to told me he would often be dragged into panel interviews for roles he had no interest or involvement in just because he was a manager (and on one occasion because he was walking past the interview room at the time).

Panel interviews can be poor screening tools because rather than having one person assess candidates through gut feel, there are now up to five people all doing the same thing. The need to coordinate several people's timetables also slows things down, so if an organisation is wedded to the panel interview concept—to recruit for positions that need multiple sign-offs, for instance—it needs to put some thought into using a process that involves a specialist recruiter, engages and inspires applicants, can be taught to all potential panel members and can be applied at high speed.

The winning combination

Organisations that use only the interview format that's most convenient or familiar to them don't realise how much they can improve their hiring success by taking the time to identify the format/s that best address their needs. For instance, boomerangs should only ever have one-on-one interviews and should never have to undergo the survivor-style contests common to group interviews. By applying the right format in the right circumstances and creating a consistent, effective system of delivery for each one, this winning combination becomes a real point of difference in the marketplace, attracting, inspiring and engaging the most talented candidates.

Assessing interviewees

In *Moneyball* conventional talent scouts assessed applicants by putting them through their paces; getting them to run, throw, field, hit and hit with power. Based on each athlete's performance on the day, along with the scout's subjective appraisal of their body shape, size and fitness, successful recruits were chosen. If a guy appeared too fat or ungainly or was just off form, he was rejected, even if his past performance showed he could catch, run or hit better than most. The selectors were feted when a few of their picks went on to become major champions, yet as Billy Beane points out, 'We take fifty guys and we celebrate if two of them make it. In what other business is two for fifty a success? If you did that in the stock market you'd go broke'.[16]

This style of 'talent scout' approach has morphed into common practice in many business organisations in which detailed hiring systems have been instituted to numerically measure people's performance *on the interview day*. Figure 5.1 and Table 5.2 give a couple of real examples of this kind of assessment.

Figure 5.1: example of an interview assessment form

At the end of the interview, circle each score that best defines the candidate:	
Personality	**1-2-3-4-5**
Intelligence	**1-2-3-4-5**
High standards	**1-2-3-4-5**
Flexibility	**1-2-3-4-5**
Sales potential	**1-2-3-4-5**
Keenness	**1-2-3-4-5**
Goal-driven	**1-2-3-4-5**
Passion for the industry	**1-2-3-4-5**
Team player	**1-2-3-4-5**
Openness and ability to learn	**1-2-3-4-5**
TOTAL/50*: _____	
*Candidates must score 35 or higher to be offered a position.	

An alternative question-based scoring system could look something like the example in table 5.2

Table 5.2: example interview questions and scoring system

Score	15	10	5	0
1 Why do you want this job?	It's a great career move.	To work for your company.	To work in this industry.	Poor answers.
2 How do you know if you've achieved in a job?	I can see measurable improvement in my results.	My manager lets me know if I've done a good job.	I know it instinctively.	Poor answers.

These two examples look like precise HR systems and they're commonly used in varying formats, but it doesn't take much to reveal their subjectivity. A colleague of mine used a derivative of the assessment form when she opened up a business in Los Angeles and thought she'd landed in recruitment heaven. All of her applicants scored 10 out of 10 on personality, keenness and so on. Within six months, however, she was embroiled in major performance management issues and her staff turnover was 65 per cent because her new people left in droves. It was only then that she realised she'd employed a lot of good-looking, personable actors and that her 'objective system' simply dressed up 'gut feel' as if it were fact.

I apologise in advance to the many companies who use this kind of format but the reality is that just because something is documented doesn't make it objective or a good system. In this case, with ill-defined elements such as 'passion' and without specific evidence-based measurement criteria, it was not only useless but actively destructive as an assessment tool.

Similarly, when I questioned the company that used the method in table 5.2, they couldn't give a scientific rationale as to why 'to work for your company' merited a 10 and 'to work in this industry' merited a 5. Even worse, the four brief responses for each question don't begin to encapsulate the many alternatives applicants may offer in an interview. When we trialled the process using different recruiters and a single interviewee, the hirers' scores varied widely, proving once again that often what looks like a rational scoring system is in fact wide open to recruiter bias.

Laszlo Bock, Vice President of People Operations at Google, a company often lauded for its comprehensive recruitment systems, shocked many when he announced a similar finding. In 2013 he said:

> *Interviews are a terrible predictor of performance.*
> *We looked at tens of thousands of interviews, and everyone who had done the interviews and what they scored the candidate, and how that person ultimately performed in their job.*
> *We found zero relationship.*
> *It's a complete random mess …*

I think many organisations could relate to this!

Exploring past performance: a key interviewing skill

These kinds of systems all have one thing in common: they all try to measure and set a numerical value on a person's performance *on the day of the interview.* If we applied this method to sport, some of the world's greatest champions renowned for getting so nervous that they throw up in advance of big games would never have been signed up.

A key interviewing skill, then, is not to try to calculate a score for a person's intrinsic make-up on the day, but rather to explore their past performance in more detail, pinpoint the attitude and behavioural patterns that underpin this tangible history, and look for a match between their *proven and demonstrated* abilities and inclinations and the job role on offer. If a person has been a high-achieving salesperson in past roles, or worked successfully in a call centre for five years, then they are a good fit for any similar role. By focusing on how people have previously performed, rather than who we think they are, recruiters make more objective decisions and transform their hiring success.

For instance, when recruiting for a manager, I once interviewed an engaging, articulate candidate who had been referred to me by the CEO. He was so charismatic that I was engrossed throughout the interview and if I'd been basing my decision on 'personality' or 'confidence', I would have hired him on the spot. It was only the next day, after the effect of his charisma had worn off, that I realised he hadn't really told me a lot about any actual workplace achievements. I rang his referee who asked me to describe the position and then said, 'I would have thought that would be a bit beyond his ability'.

Top tips for interviewing

To accurately examine past performance a recruiter needs to create a set of definitive interview questions. I've trialled a lot of these and by analysing the people who stayed and the ones who left, I've been able to work out which are most effective. I've included a sample interview later in this chapter. But first, here are my top general tips for success.

Use only relevant questions, and don't use too many

Recruiters often justify their positions by including masses of questions in their interviews and this is a real turn-off to applicants. Every question should have a specific purpose—if not, axe it. The recruiter then has time to probe a candidate's specific answers for more detail on past performance or attitudes, as the need arises.

Make the questions stimulating

Make the interview process an engaging exchange, rather than a meaningless interaction, by asking questions that resonate with people. For instance, when I began asking applicants, 'What do you see as your greatest achievement in life?' it took the conversation to a whole new level, one where people could see that the organisation was genuinely interested in them, not just looking for robotic answers.

Use the same standard questions in every interview for the same role

I found that by asking the same questions in every interview, I could determine the statistical relevance of the replies. For instance, I found that those candidates who said they hated their manager in answer to my question, 'What do you like least about your current job?' had a turnover rate of 40 per cent. Those who gave this answer and were also negative about other work relationships when talking about their life in the first question increased the risk to 80 per cent.

An interview, then, is not a haphazard process in which the employer asks any question off the top of their head. It's a selection of proven, effective questions combined in an order that keeps an applicant inspired and challenged. When I'm consulting, clients often tell me, 'Oh, yeah, we use questions like that,' but when I examine further they've usually just thrown a few together, like ingredients in a pot, and—most critically—never measured them for effectiveness.

A sample interview process

So that's the theory. Now here's an example of a one-on-one interview process, one that I've designed, trialled and perfected over many years and in many organisations. It consists of the following steps:

1 Introduction.

2 Key questions on past performance, attitude and practical fit.

3 Skills and qualifications questions.

4 Selling the benefits of the role and the organisation.

5 Trial close.

6 Setting expectations.

Introduction

Like any good relationship, the first step in the process is an effective introduction. This is where the recruiter gives a brief potted history of their own journey with the organisation, and inspires applicants with the benefits they've experienced, such as career advancement or job satisfaction. This is another reason why non-achievers make poor recruiters—they have no inspiring story to tell.

The second purpose of the introduction is to give the candidate an overview of the interview format. By letting them know that they can ask all their questions at the end, the recruiter doesn't get side-tracked during the assessment process. It saves time because by then they'll have answered most of the candidate's queries in the 'selling the benefits' section. For instance:

> *I'll begin by asking you a few questions about yourself, then I'll tell you a bit more about the business and the role we're recruiting for. At the end, if you have any questions that we haven't covered, we can go through those.*

This is also the time to assess physical appearance. I'm not interested in what candidates wear, but rather whether they have made an effort, as that demonstrates commitment. People dress in their best for an interview, so if they are looking sloppy now, they will look a lot worse as a new recruit. If the position is one in which the interviewee will be face-to-face with clients, then this aspect carries more weight than for a role behind the scenes.

Key questions

The next step of the interview consists of questions designed to reveal the candidate's attitudes, values, likes and dislikes, as well as any practical information required to make a successful offer. I approach every interview like a voyage of discovery because I want to find out as much as I can about a person's background to uncover what lies below their surface answers. This is as essential for the applicant as it is for me. If I employ a candidate whose attitudes and skills are a poor match for the role, then I'm wasting not only my organisation's time, money and resources, but the candidate's as well.

Remember that these questions are only useful when used as a yardstick to compare answers with past performance. The discrepancies reveal when candidates are genuine versus just telling me what I want to hear. Jotting down actual candidate examples and phrases on a blank interview questionnaire will also help to make the final assessment.

Here's a set of questions I often use.

Tell me about yourself

Starting with an open-ended question relaxes people and stymies those who have been coached to give pat answers to standard interview questions. What applicants *choose* to tell you can also be revealing. Those who have an attitude of openness and are quite happy to talk about their job history have been my best recruits. Closed candidates, who jump straight to their existing role and wrap this question up in a couple of sentences, have always been my poorest recruits.

This highlights that a candidate's manner of answering is often more important than what they say. Do they present their life experiences in a positive or negative light? Do they externalise their problems? Do they demonstrate perseverance? What have they achieved? Do they talk in a positive or negative manner about their people interactions? What is their attitude to work? Do their answers gel with the work history demonstrated on their CV?

I ask clarifying questions as they talk—for instance, 'You left university part-way through your degree. What was the reason for that?', or 'What made you decide to change careers?' so that by the end I have a general overview of their attitudes, values, skills and experience. I also write down actual statements and phrases they use that reflect any of my top five attitudes—a positive work ethic, perseverance, achievement, no people conflict and commitment. This helps me to make a good recruitment decision. For example, I may have the following written down:

- 'I wasn't great at school.'

- 'Mum wouldn't pay for me to go to university.'

- 'I hate my job.'

- 'A new owner has taken over and I just don't like what he's doing.'

Compare this pattern of negativity to the following statements, which illustrate perseverance and achievement:

- 'I worked at the local fish and chip shop when I was 16 so I could save up to buy my first car.'

- 'My first boss was pretty old-school but I stuck it out because I knew I could learn a lot there.'

- 'I like my job, but I've been there for five years now so I'm looking for a new challenge.'

Of course these statements are only valid if the attitudes demonstrated are also backed up by historical evidence. If the applicant who made the negative statements also demonstrated in their work record a pattern of disrupted job history, then they would be a definite 'no'.

Give me an example of something you consider to be a good work ethic

This question looks at people's fundamental attitudes to working life. People who enjoy work and are positive about it make good recruits. Good answers to this question include, 'Always do a good job', or 'Give 100 per cent to whatever you do'. Bad responses include the applicant struggling to answer the question or giving a reply such as, 'Try and show up on time, I suppose'. You'd think that no-one would be this thoughtless, yet in practice I've found that because this question is just outside the box, it produces revealing results.

What do you like most about your current job?

This helps determine whether the position is a good fit for the applicant. There's no point employing a candidate with great qualifications and past achievements if there's something they'll hate about the position. For example, if the thing they liked the most was the teamwork and the advertised role is a stand-alone position, then the fit is not great. This is also why it's essential for the recruiter to understand the core physical requirements of a role or they won't make a good match.

What do you like least about your current job?

I ask this for the same reason as the question above. If they hate long hours and your position is time-intensive, then they're a bad fit. These types of practical-fit questions also allow me to explore discrepancies. If a candidate says they hate long hours but they have worked in jobs with long hours for the past 15 years, it's important to probe further to find out *why* they've changed their tune for this position.

Why are you looking to leave your current employer?

This question assesses their motivation for applying. A good answer is that they really like their current employer/job but have hit a ceiling and there's no more opportunity for them to grow there. If they hate their job and are desperate to get out of it, they may be applying for anything and everything and may not be committed to this position. This question also creates another piece of evidence to use as a yard-stick when reference-checking.

What was it that attracted you to the advertised position?

This is another commitment question. Good signs are if they have researched the job and company and/or have a rational reason for their application. If they applied on a whim, their answers are along the lines of 'the fashion industry sounds really glamorous so I thought I'd give it a shot'. The best answers demonstrate some history of wanting to work in this field, or with this company, perhaps through mentioning other similar positions they've applied for.

What do you see as the greatest achievement in your life?

I love this question. It helps me connect with people in a real sense, not just in a surface manner. It's often an interview turning point for good applicants, especially after the other, more standard, questions. It signals that the recruiter is genuinely looking for people to make a difference to the organisation, not just filling vacancies.

It also reveals a candidate's underlying attitude towards achievement. People's responses often surprise me, such as the applicant who'd been self-effacing throughout the interview and then said, 'I won an Olympic medal'.

Natural achievers light up and readily answer this question with objective and merit-based detail such as, 'I won my company's top sales award two years in a row', or 'I became a manager in less than 12 months'. Some break into stories about football, travel or ballet.

Low-achieving candidates often struggle to answer. One 45-year-old candidate told me, after several minutes of thought, that the greatest achievement in his life was 'getting his driver's licence'. Another applicant sat straight up and very seriously said, 'I'm sorry. I haven't prepared for that question'.

If someone answers with a general achievement such as, 'the birth of my two children', I then ask them what their greatest career achievement is. Remember this question is only useful if an organisation wants someone to develop in a role. If the position is one with little possibility of growth or promotion, then it's a bad fit for an achiever.

What was the toughest hurdle you've had to face and how did you deal with it?

This question assesses not only a candidate's attitude to perseverance but also their definition of what constitutes an obstacle. If their greatest hurdle was simply a standard part of life, then this is a bad sign. I'm not so interested in their solutions, only what they consider difficult and whether they stuck it out or cut and run.

What do you see as your strengths/weaknesses?

Many people are prepared for or have been coached in this kind of question, but what they don't know is that it's a reality check. The point is to see if their answer matches the demonstrated evidence that's been collected. For instance, if someone has demonstrated a repeated inability to get along with people with comments such as, 'I left school because there was a teacher I didn't see eye to eye with', 'My first boss was a pig', or 'My current manager doesn't listen to my ideas' and then says their strength is in the way they connect with people, they're an unsuitable recruit for most roles. In my experience, a person's self-awareness is in direct proportion to their effectiveness and ability to learn.

Where do you see yourself in five years' time?

This question tests their commitment. The best answers are those that show growth and development in the role, and that the candidate has thought about a future with the organisation. 'Becoming the number-one salesperson', or 'At management level here' are good answers.

These sound rehearsed but I'm often surprised at the honest responses I get to this question. One candidate looked at me and said, 'I'm hoping to get a job as an air hostess with Virgin Airlines and I thought this job would be a good stepping stone'.

Apart from applicants who are very young, those who have a hazy view of their future are high-risk candidates. If you're recruiting for a plumber and they see themselves maybe working on a cruise ship or running their own hair salon, then they have no commitment to a future with you. Personal goals are good as they demonstrate openness. If someone says they'd like to have a house and a couple of kids, this is a positive answer because the person is being honest with me. 'In your job!' is also a good answer.

If you weren't successful for this position, what other roles would you apply for?

This again tests their commitment. If they're looking for roles similar to the one you're advertising, then they're serious about this position. If they're toying with many different job ideas, then they're higher risk because they haven't worked out what they really want. This is also a good question for finding out what other interviews really good candidates have in the pipeline. The recruiter can have an open discussion with them on this so they know the time frame for a job offer.

What are your salary expectations? (What are you currently earning?)

If the applicant is good you need this information to know what to offer and whether you're even in their ballpark on salary. You don't need to take it as gospel, as some people will lie, but it will be indicative. I prefer to ask straight out, but an alternative to this question is, 'What would be your dream job?' This is useful if you're operating in a tight labour market. If you want an even more holistic picture, you can also put these kinds of 'buying' criteria questions on a pre-screening questionnaire that the candidate fills out before the interview. As well as helping with the creation of a compelling job offer, these answers can also be used to collate a KPI sheet to address unrealistic beliefs on salary competitiveness at an executive level.

If you were successful, when would you be available to start?

This is practical information needed to help with planning, should the applicant prove suitable for the position.

When I contact your referees, what do you think they'll say about you?

This sets up the reference check, as you can then compare their answers with those of the referees and note any discrepancies. As I will outline in chapter 6, I use many of the same questions with the referee as I do in the interview so that I can directly compare the results. The use of 'when' in this question is also critical as it sends a strong message to give honest answers.

Skills and qualifications

Once the recruiter has an overview of the applicant's suitability, they can assess their skills and qualifications and ensure they align with the declared past performance. Checking certificates and other qualifications by sight is vital and then, if the role is for a technical position, the recruiter can hand over to the line manager to assess the candidate's skills in this area: 'Now I'll hand you over to David, who is going to ask you some questions about your technical skills'.

Otherwise they can assess the candidate's actual skills themselves through stimulating questioning, exercises, tests, role plays or simulations. Whatever assessment an organisation chooses, it must be specific enough so that candidates' results can be compared in an objective, useful fashion.

Some forms of assessment, such as a numeric reasoning test to determine mathematical ability or online simulations, can be scheduled on the interview day if the results are necessary for making a good decision. Don't go over the top in assessment, though. When I went undercover at the yachting company I had to sit a typing speed test, even though this wasn't integral to my recruitment skills. (I failed, but they employed me anyway.) Organisations often subject candidates to batteries of tests, but when I question them, many are unable to tell me how they can apply any of this information to the recruitment decision-making process. IQ tests, for instance, are useless because straight intelligence, without people skills or practical application, often has little correlation with job success.

Sometimes after questioning and testing, there's a gap between the position requirements and the candidate's skills and qualifications, so this is when the following question is handy, in the spirit of fairness:

- 'One of my concerns with your application is that you don't have any _____' (experience in driving a forklift, for example).

- 'If I had two applicants — yourself and another person with that experience — what reasons can you give me as to why I should offer you this position?'

This gives them an opportunity to address this disadvantage and come up with a *rational* reason to convince the recruiter that they're the best person for the position. Gushing enthusiasm is not an adequate response here.

This question also helps unsuitable candidates understand why they're not a good fit for the role, which softens the blow when they get the 'no' letter. One applicant said to me in answer to this question, 'You know, you're right. I wouldn't give me this job either'. We shook hands and she went off to find a position that did suit her.

Selling the benefits

'That's all the questions I wanted to ask you. Now I'll tell you a bit more about the position and about our organisation.'

The candidate will already have a first impression of the business based on the pre-interview phone call, correspondence and onsite reception. Now it's time for the recruiter to sell the benefits and points of difference face-to-face, using such tools as I've already outlined. Placing this step after the interview questions can save a lot of time for both the applicant and the hirer because if the candidate is obviously a poor fit for the role, then this becomes a brief overview. If the recruiter has determined that the candidate may be suitable, however, then they can spend a lot of time on this. I then ask, 'Do you have any questions about any areas that I may not have covered?'

Look for questions that reveal buying signs—that is, positive indications that the candidate is interested in the job and/or is looking at long-term commitment. For instance:

- 'So if I did well in my first year, I could become a manager then?'

- 'I like the sound of your mentoring program. How long do I need to work for the company before I can apply for this?'

The direction of their questions will give the recruiter more evidence of their attitudes and whether they're a good fit. If the candidate asks a lot of questions relating to flexibility of hours and the job role is very inflexible, then the position is probably not right for them. I've also found that candidates who whip out a notebook at this point and ask a litany of overly detailed questions with little relevance to the position never make good employees. If the recruiter has done a good job, and the applicant doesn't appear interested or engaged at this stage, then walk away. They may be a great candidate, but if the recruiter feels they have to convince them to take the job, it means they're not a good fit as they're unmoved by the benefits that have been outlined to them.

The trial close

All good salespeople know that a trial close is crucial. The candidate is now clear about what's involved with the job. If the recruiter thinks, at this point, that they may be suitable, then they need to find out if *the applicant* is still interested in the position. After years of selling I discovered the best way to do this is simply by asking them, 'Does this sound like the sort of position you're looking for?'

This question will elicit any doubts or objections the applicant may have and gives the recruiter a chance to address them. For instance:

Candidate: *'It sounds like this job involves a bit more travelling than I'm used to.'*

Recruiter: *'There is a lot of travelling in the first three months, as you meet everyone, but after this period you'd only be jetting off for two days in every eight weeks.'*

Once again, look for positive buying signs such as, 'It sounds ideal', or 'I really like the sound of your training program'. Hesitancy or non-committal responses such as, 'I'd have to think it over a bit' mean the candidate is statistically likely to reject a job offer.

A recruiter should *never, ever* omit the trial close, otherwise they'll have no idea where the candidate stands or whether their job offer will be successful. It helps with planning because if the applicant sounds disinterested, the organisation can immediately begin considering other possibilities.

Setting expectations

The final step in the interview is to set clear expectations so the candidate knows what happens next and where to go with any queries in the interim. If the candidate proves suitable, the recruiter can then make a job offer as soon as the following day.

Once the interview has ended and the applicant has left, the recruiter needs to take a few minutes to record their general thoughts and example statements, otherwise they will find that after a dozen interviews they can't remember the exact ins and outs of each candidate. The decision as to whether the candidate is suitable or not is best left until the following day (see chapter 6).

Measure, measure, measure

The ultimate success of an interview process can be directly measured by the number of dropouts post interview and changes in the recruitment conversion rate. If the dropouts start increasing and the conversion rate decreasing, a good strategy is to get interviewees who turn over to fill out a confidential questionnaire. That way the organisation can determine which aspect of the business or the interview process is the root cause of the problem and make improvements.

Another way to measure the recruiter's actual interview performance is the 'Mystery Shopper' concept. Hirers can get burned out from conducting too many interviews and this indifference comes across clearly to an applicant. By sending in a test applicant to evaluate the hirer on the five criteria for great recruiters (which we covered in chapter 2), a company can identify when they need to take some time out from hiring to recover from this kind of lethargy. Making this strategy a standard part of the system also inspires recruiters to operate at peak performance during every interview.

Key components of great interviews

Figure 5.2 outlines the key components of an effective interview system.

Figure 5.2: the key components of interviewing

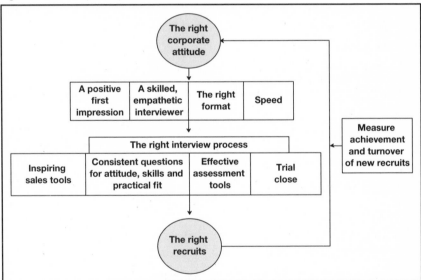

Interviewing is one area that really benefits from being put under the microscope. By challenging conventional wisdom, hypothesising and meticulously testing against the evidence, an organisation can take huge strides forward in its hiring success. Billy Beane summed this up—after dumping his subjective interviewing practices and adopting objective, measurable processes—when he said, 'However we do it we're never going to be more wrong than the way we did it before'.[17]

Interviewing techniques

Use the following questions to assess how your organisation could improve its interviewing techniques.

→ Do our interviews inspire as well as assess applicants?

→ What sort of first impression do applicants receive when they arrive for an interview?

→ How do our recruiters build a positive relationship with interviewees?

→ Who's involved in conducting our interviews? Do they need to be involved? Does this impact on speed and, if so, how can this be improved on?

→ On a scale of 1 to 10 with 1 being the worst and 10 being the best, how would we rate our interviews in the following areas?

- o Inspiring venue.

- o Effective interview formats.

- o Consistent, standard questions on attitude, skills and practical fit.

- o Objective measurement to determine the usefulness of currently used questions.

- o Objective and challenging skills assessment questions, tests or exercises.

- o Consistent standard tools that sell the organisational and role benefits.

→ Do our recruiters record actual examples of evidence of attitude throughout the interview?

→ Do they trial close every applicant?

→ How do we measure our post-interview drop-outs?

→ How do we measure our recruiters' performances in interviews?

CHAPTER 6

Engaging: employing the best people for the business

We don't like their sound, and guitar music is on the way out.
Decca Recording Company rejecting the Beatles, 1962

Fred Astaire can't act, can't sing, balding... can dance a little.
MGM talent scout, 1928

What can you do with a guy with ears like that?
Jack Warner, movie mogul, rejecting Clark Gable, 1930

I'm always fascinated by the way people make recruitment decisions. My first manager employed strangers he met in the pub and liked. An HR person I worked with when I was 19 recruited people with hard-luck stories because she felt sorry for them and wanted to give them a new start in life. A friend of mine only employs people who are dressed well in the interview because 'clothes tell you a lot about a person'. These recruiters all place emotional or intuitive selection processes above logical reasoning.

Some employers go to the other extreme with techniques that are overtly systematic. They make their decision based on the results of a battery of personality tests in the belief that it's possible to distil the unknowable complexities of human nature into a graded rating that can be used to compare candidates. This is dubious methodology because if there were a test that could cure all of our recruitment ills, we'd be using it in every aspect of our lives such as picking our spouses, our business partners and our life-long friends.

Making a good decision then, is more difficult than it first appears. When I first started recruiting I worked on 'gut instinct'. The first person I ever employed was Jack, a charismatic musician. I interviewed him in a coffee shop and loved his infectious enthusiasm. In fact, I liked him so much I offered him a job as a travel agent, on the spot. He started the next day. I didn't get to spend much time with him in his first week because we were really busy, so I was shocked when he came to me on the Friday afternoon and told me he didn't think the job was for him.

'But Jack,' I said. 'You told me it was the perfect role for you. That you'd never wanted anything more.'

'Yep,' he shrugged, 'I guess I was wrong. I don't really like having to deal with people all day. I met a bloke in the pub last night and he reckons I can make a lot of money singing on cruise ships so I've decided to give that a go instead'.

I was devastated, but I learned from this experience that 'gut instinct' is a poor decision-making tool and that enthusiasm without commitment means nothing when it comes to hiring.

Creating a shortlist

This episode also made me appreciate the benefits of creating an objective shortlist. From then on, I used actual proof, which I gathered from cover letters/emails, CVs, interviews and other interactions, to fill out an assessment checklist that was helpful in comparing one applicant with another in an empirical manner. I never did this on the same day as the interview because someone's charisma might blind me to objective evidence, but after 24 hours I could view the candidates rationally and write down all the tangible points. You can see my assessment checklist in figure 6.1.

Figure 6.1: candidate assessment checklist

Name	Positive	Perseverance	Achievement	No people conflict	Commitment	OVERALL ATTITUDE	Education	Customer service	Sales	Management	OVERALL SKILLS	Practical fit	OVERALL FIT	YES/NO

This checklist makes it obvious if someone is a standout, in which case I may simply reference check them. If I have some question marks about their application, or I don't feel I have enough evidence to reach a verdict on one of the checklist criteria, I give them the benefit of the doubt and do further vetting before making a final decision.

Vetting shortlisted candidates

Here are the tools I've found the most effective for vetting shortlisted candidates.

Ring the applicant

If on reflection, post interview, I have an area of concern, I ring the applicant and raise it directly with them. The advantage of this approach is that if they have a logical response and I end up employing them, they will do everything possible to prove me wrong regarding my area of concern, which neutralises future problems.

Further testing

This can be anything from aptitude tests to determine skills such as numerical or verbal reasoning, to post-interview psychometric tests. You may have gleaned that I'm not a big fan of the latter. This is not because of the tests per se, but simply because too many organisations use them as a crutch for their entire hiring decision without any objective evidence as to their effectiveness. One renowned provider, whose test was used by a number of large multinational organisations, admitted to me under cross examination that he'd made the questions up. They had no statistical validity at all.

Even organisations that are reputable can produce poor hiring results. My company introduced a test that was approved by the well-respected British Psychologists Association, but over time the quality of our recruits diminished and they began to turn over. On analysis, we found that the test was knocking out candidates who didn't demonstrate constant 'high energy'. This seemed like good sense because all organisations want energetic candidates. When we tested our existing highest achievers—who were hired before we introduced this test—however, they all failed this aspect because they operated more like sprinters with periods of high and low energy. In this case our assessment tool had been actively screening out our best possible recruits—those with both high and low energy levels—for months.

We approached the company that provided the test and they pointed out that all these potential variables were detailed in the fine print in their complex, 300-page user manual. This highlighted to me another downside to these tests, which is that most people applying them are not trained or expert in their use.

From an applicant's point of view, it's also easy to cheat on a psychometric test. A quick Google search comes up with actual answers and numerous websites that school people on the best way to pass with flying colours. There are books, DVDs, guides and even tutors for this service. This is an ominous development for any company that bases all its decision-making on such tools.

My hiring mantra, then, is that:

> *The best use of psychometric tests is as an adjunct to the*
> *recruitment process.*

For example, if I've identified objective evidence during an interview that a candidate has conflicted with people in past roles, and the psychometric test also rates them high on confrontation, then I would make the decision to reject their application. Where there's a disparity, however, I would always put more weight on my actual collected evidence.

Work experience

This is one of the best vetting tools. When I introduced a two-hour stint of work experience in a retail shop as part of my hiring process, my new staff turnover dropped by a whopping 40 per cent. I put this down to the fact that the recruiter gets to assess how a candidate responds to real-life scenarios. Some applicants who had been brilliant in the interview fell apart when faced with five phones ringing non-stop in an office. They thought they'd be good at selling travel, but all they were good at was travelling. It's also a great test of the candidate's commitment. Because it takes time, anyone who is lukewarm about the job will drop out before undergoing this process.

In practice, applicants generally like work experience because they get to talk to existing employees and see and feel the work environment, warts and all, to determine whether it suits them. As painful as it is to lose a great applicant, it's better for them to drop out of the process at this point than a few months later when it costs a lot more in time, money and morale to replace them. Because the existing employees feel they've been involved in the recruitment process they also take a lot more ownership of the new person, which means they're warm, welcoming and helpful when the recruit starts in the role.

Once again, speed is relevant when it comes to work experience so if possible, arrange it for the same day as the interview so the applicant only has to take time off work once. It doesn't have to be long—even an hour is useful—but it does need to be structured. When I first started doing them, the applicants simply sat in a store for two hours making coffee and doing photocopying, and often complained that the employees were too busy to assess them in any way. In response, we re-trained our people so that these potential recruits experienced a genuine welcome. I also put together some exercises that the applicants could do themselves so they felt challenged and engaged by the process regardless of how busy the employees were at the time.

Reference and background checks

I never used to do reference checks. My screening process seemed to work and when I did ring referees they were always positive about candidates, so I never learned anything of use. At that stage I thought no-one would be silly enough to provide a referee who would give them a bad reference. Then I recruited for a company where reference checks were compulsory. I was forced to do them and made a unique discovery: people *are* silly enough!

For instance, I said to one referee that I was concerned because the person's achievements on their CV didn't seem to match up with the calibre of the candidate I'd interviewed. In other words, I was suggesting they were lying. The referee, who had offered only general niceties about the candidate up to this point, then said, 'You appear to be a woman of good business sense. I would go with that gut feeling if I were you'.

When it comes to reference checks I look for congruency between what the applicant says and what the referee says. Many of the questions I ask the referee as a standard—you will find my checklist in figure 6.2—are exactly the same as my interview questions. I then compare the two responses and note any outstanding discrepancies.

Figure 6.2: reference check questionnaire

REFERENCE CHECK QUESTIONNAIRE

NAME: _____
DATE: _____
POSITION APPLIED FOR: _____

REFERENCE RATING: (Circle one)   POOR   AVERAGE   EXCELLENT

1   Why did you employ the candidate?

2   How did they measure up to that first impression?

3   What were their greatest achievements in the role?

4   What do you see that may let them down in a work environment?

5   How would you compare their performance with others in the same role?

6   How would you describe their relationship with other employees? Clients?

7   On a scale of 1 to 5 with 1 being the worst and 5 being the best, how would you rate them for:
    Honesty and integrity?   ___
    Perseverance?   ___
    Positive attitude?   ___
    Drive and motivation?   ___
    Team interaction?   ___

8   Why did they leave your organisation?

9   Would you re-employ them if the opportunity arose?

10 Do you think their attributes and skills are suitable for success in this particular role?

11 Is there anything I haven't covered that you think would be useful to know?

I do deviate from this checklist. Nowadays everyone is a bit more politically correct because of the fear of litigation, so I've found I often have to dig more when I feel people are hedging. Referees are reluctant to stymie a person's chances, but I find if I keep asking the same question in a number of different ways, their desire for truthfulness eventually wins out.

Sometimes—if I only have one area of concern—I may only have one question for a referee. Employers or recruiters who assail a referee with hundreds of questions are often compensating for ineffective screening processes in the vain hope that a complete stranger will make the assessment for them. Good recruiters make a preliminary judgement based on objective evidence and then use the reference check to test that decision.

There are other background checks you can use to confirm people's credentials. Many employers search the internet and people's Facebook pages to check up on potential employees. This can be very revealing, especially when the information posted contrasts with the personal details they gave in the interview. For instance, in one high-profile court case in Australia, a US surgeon who was charged with manslaughter and grievous bodily harm after a number of patient deaths and disabilities had his prior surgical practice bans uncovered by a journalist who typed his name into a random search engine.

The final factor to consider when it comes to any type of background check is again speed in the hiring process. You can't let it stall while conducting these checks as a good candidate will be getting other offers all the time. If an applicant scores well in all criteria, but because the chief referee is away on holidays the decision can't be tested, I would always take a punt and employ them without a reference check rather than risk losing them.

If other checks are necessary to fulfil corporate policy, my advice is to employ the person but make very clear in the discussion before the appointment (and highlight in the employment contract) that a negative report in eight weeks' time will lead to instant dismissal. In my experience, this is enough to prompt any unsuitable applicants to drop out of the process at this stage.

Making the final decision

Once recruiters have tested their shortlisted candidates using some or all of the above tools, they're ready to make the final decision. This is where the checklist comes in handy. Here are the possible outcomes.

- *100 per cent for attitude, skills and fit.* The good candidates stand out like beacons — good assessments, reference checks and pass marks on work experience or testing — so circle them straight away. If you only have one position, but several candidates have scored 100 per cent across all criteria, take the one with the highest education level and the most demonstrated achievement as they will have the least turnover risk.

- *100 per cent for attitude, but not for skills and/or fit.* If you don't get anyone who has scored 100 per cent in the skill and fit assessments, see whether any are salvageable. Perhaps they could learn the skills they're missing. Maybe you can make an alternative offer involving flexibility or brightness of future that may get you over the 'too expensive' salary hurdle. In a tight labour market, where the standout candidates are limited, this type of creative approach is often necessary just to fill vacancies.

- *100 per cent for skills and fit, but not for attitude.* When should a company compromise its choice of candidates if they have a poor attitude? The answer is never! Well almost. There are simply no roles in which a negative work ethic, constant people conflict, a lack of perseverance or minimal commitment can be counted as an asset. Employing candidates with poor attitudes will fill vacancies, but the damage caused by meagre results, constant performance management, low staff morale and continual turnover is worse than the original problem of unfilled vacancies. Add in the dollar cost of turnover at 50 per cent to 150 per cent of the annual wage, and a bad recruitment decision can be one of the most costly errors a business will make.

Often the reason an organisation is under intense pressure to fill a position is because they've gone through the whole recruitment process several times and still don't have any suitable candidates.

Yet this is almost always because of poor recruitment processes in the first place, such as—for example—ineffective advertising; not moving quickly enough; not selling the benefits of the role and the organisation; or limiting the target market to people with skills rather than recruiting for attitude. Sometimes it can be a combination of many of these factors.

I was once called in as a consultant to help an organisation recruit a manager. They had been advertising the position for eight weeks with no success, primarily because the person recruiting was also managing two other operations and hadn't made the hiring a priority. In fact he'd hardly looked at a single CV. As the existing manager was leaving in a fortnight, the business was desperate to fill the vacancy.

This is what I call 'miracle' recruitment, but I decided to give it a whirl. I went back over all of the CVs and found three great applicants. I rang them, but after eight weeks they all had other positions. I moved to Plan B. There was a candidate who rated as an 'ideal' manager on the organisation's psychometric test. He was high risk on people conflict and lacked demonstrated achievement according to my attitude assessment. In a normal process I would never have recruited him. In this case we had no choice—it was employ him or shut the business down—so, as he was available to start immediately, we took a chance on him.

This achieved the goal of keeping the business running but at a very high cost. The manager was argumentative, conflicted repeatedly with the existing staff, was the subject of repeated customer complaints and after months of performance management was eventually sacked. This whole situation could have been avoided if the organisation had simply moved quickly and followed a good recruitment process in the first place. They had had three suitable applicants but they hadn't screened them properly or followed them up in time. I became the scapegoat because I'd employed the final candidate, which taught me a valuable lesson about last-minute 'miracle' recruitment: the applicants will always be high risk because you're always forced to lower the recruitment criteria to fill the position on time.

The final two reality checks

Once an employer has identified a suitable candidate to fill a position there are two final reality checks that need to be applied: recruiter bias and gut instinct.

Recruiter bias

Every HR person has an inclination towards or against a certain type of person. My friend Alicia employed very attractive male applicants, in spite of any contrary evidence. Another recruiter I knew never employed young people, particularly if they had nose rings. Rugby players employ rugby players. Dog lovers hire other dog lovers. These biases can and do mask many attributes that may be incompatible with good recruitment.

It doesn't matter what the bias is; the main thing is to recognise it and compensate for it. Every recruiter should be open about their inclination so that they can be extra rigorous in analysing the applications of those who fit into this category. Even better is if they can offload the applicant to another recruiter to assess. I used to do this with a colleague in the UK, which was fairer for the candidate and gave us more successful recruitment outcomes.

Gut instinct

I have found that if I've conducted all my objective assessments and addressed recruiter bias and I'm still ambivalent about someone, there's usually a good reason—even if I can't articulate it. In the past I often employed people despite my gut instinct and had 100 per cent turnover.

Now is the only time I trust my gut instinct. I may not be able to put it into definitive terms, but if someone has not convinced me of their suitability in the interview and I remain uncertain about them after all my objective screening and testing, then the answer is always 'no'.

Making an inspiring job offer

Okay, you've now got a great candidate in your sights and you want to hire them. Like hooking a fish and actually getting it into the boat, however, making an offer and getting it accepted are two very different things. I had a great example of how poor recruitment processes can affect the outcome of a job offer when a client asked me to sit in on an interview for an IT position. The candidate answered my attitudinal questions well and was a suitable match for the role. When I passed him over to the recruiter to talk about the position and the company, however, she rambled on for 20 minutes about corporate history and didn't sell a single benefit. She made the company sound boring and bureaucratic when the reality was the exact opposite. It then took her more than a week to convince the applicant to take the position and she ended up paying $15 000 more than the original salary on offer. Because she'd missed out one fundamental step of the process—articulating the benefits—it was very difficult to close the sale.

This is where the first five steps of my Highfliers 7-step System come into their own. If the recruiter has handled the applicant well, built good rapport, been dynamic and engaging in the interview, sold the objective benefits of the role and the organisation, and moved with speed throughout the process, the candidate is already thinking, 'This is my employer of choice'. Rather than being a hard sell as in the example above, engaging the applicant is now a natural, logical stage in the process, akin to water flowing downhill.

The Highfliers pre-interview checklist and targeted interview questions also help because they ensure recruiters already have a clear understanding of a specific individual's needs. This enables them to put together a winning offer that matches the person's requirements and/or highlights the features of the organisation that align with their needs, so that closing 'the sale' becomes a lot easier.

There are a few other factors that can give you a competitive edge when making an offer.

Personalise the offer

By personalising the offer, you increase the number of candidates that accept positions. When I was recruiting for a management couple in a remote location, our best candidates already had a number of job offers on the table. The front-runners liked our role but we knew we had to come up with a real point of difference to clinch the deal.

Because they had a small child, we decided to include one day a week free babysitting in the salary package. They were so impressed that we'd considered their personal circumstances and tailor-made the package around them that they took the job and started with a lot of goodwill towards the organisation.

Always ring with the offer

Being offered a job is an exciting moment in a person's life. Organisations tend to forget this and treat many successful applicants as if they're simply cogs in a machine. Yet the manner of the offer can directly influence whether someone takes a job or not. Never email or post an acceptance letter as it's much harder to convey excitement and a sense of achievement through these media. They often come across as dry and boring, such as this example of an actual letter I came across.

Dear _____,

We wish to advise that you have been successful in your application for the advertised role. Please fill out the 10-page contract enclosed and post it back to our administrations centre within seven days. Your induction will be on the 2nd of September at 9 am. Please wear closed-in shoes to comply with our workplace health and safety regulations. We will issue you with your employee number on arrival and you must wear your employee badge at all times. If you have any questions, ring _____.

Yours sincerely,

If I'd been the successful recruit I would have run a mile.

Compare that letter to a phone call with the following message.

'Hi, it's Mandy here. As you know we had over 100 people apply for this position and many of them were exceptional applicants. You were one of the people to make it through to the short list. We sat down yesterday and assessed all the candidates on our list and, after giving it a lot of thought, we believe that you are the best applicant. We would like to offer you the position.'

In this age of increasing technology many see the use of phone calls as outdated, yet for those in the 'people' business this kind of genuine personal interaction is vital.

Time the offer for maximum success

Some employers are so keen to sign up a candidate that they finish their interview by saying, 'Well, the job's yours if you want it'. This is the worst thing a recruiter can do. Not only does it smack of desperation, but it also undermines the applicant's sense of achievement in getting the position. They will think to themselves, 'It must be a lemon if he's so desperate that he's not even stopping to think it over. Maybe no-one else has even applied'. It's far better to ring the applicant the next day and offer them the position, creating a sense of achievement, as in the example above.

Speed, speed and more speed

Once again, speed is essential when it comes to the offer process. If a recruiter is obliged to wait for the result of other interviews, then it's important that they keep in contact with the preferred applicant to let them know how the process is going. This gives them advance notice of any competing job offers and also enables them to keep building rapport, which makes a good contrast to the impersonal approaches of other organisations.

It's crucial to get the contract back quickly because once someone has physically signed, they're mentally off the market and will stop job hunting. In my early days of recruitment I was satisfied with a verbal commitment and lost a few good candidates because of my inexperience. If people aren't willing to sign—or delay signing—it usually means they're still toying with other options and are unlikely to commit to the role on offer.

Follow up

Follow up your offer with a personalised contract and a warm welcome letter. Once the applicant has agreed to the details, such as salary and start date, make sure the follow-up letter and contract for them to peruse and sign are personal and welcoming.

How to say 'no'

Every good recruiter needs to learn how to manage unsuccessful candidates well, especially when poor handling can lead to litigation. This is easy when an applicant doesn't meet some aspect of the selection criteria or when the successful recruit is demonstratively more qualified. In these cases, I outline this in an objective manner and find the conversations are generally positive.

It can be tricky, however, when there are a large number of suitable applicants and the final decision simply comes down to the best organisational or team fit. When I started recruiting I was very idealistic and wanted to help everyone, so when someone rang to find out why they didn't get a position, I always explained the closeness of the race and then suggested ways they could improve their next application. Here are the types of responses I received.

> *'I don't think the fact that I had slightly less sales experience has anything to do with it. I noticed your Croydon office had three women working there so I think you just don't like men.' (In my defence I would just like to point out that my company at this time was 75 per cent male.)*

> *'Are you sure that's the reason or is it because I'm too old? I've talked to the Equal Opportunities Commission and they told me it was discrimination if anyone knocks me back because of my age.'*

I discovered that many people weren't ringing because they wanted to know how they could improve themselves, but rather to vent their feelings of displeasure and rejection for not getting the job.

After the experiences of being verbally abused and threatened, I decided to adopt a more pragmatic approach. I now tell everyone in this category that they were just pipped at the post by someone else. It's not as helpful, but it means I don't venture into dangerous areas of liability with people determined to portray me as an evil recruiter out to unfairly destroy their lives.

The way a recruiter handles unsuccessful applicants can also directly impact on a corporation's branding. If a recruiter contacts someone, via phone or interview, and then the candidate never hears from them again, it creates a poor impression. The applicant is less likely to want any further dealings with that organisation, either as a client or as an applicant in future. This is especially important to note because the successful candidate may still drop out at this stage. One of mine did after signing his contract, after he was involved in an accident. Because I'd handled the process well, it was easy for me to go back to one of my other suitable candidates and make a late job offer.

It's all about respect, remembering that you're dealing with people and feelings, not numbers. If a company is large and gets inundated with CVs for every job ad, the best approach is to advise in the ad that only successful applicants will be notified. That way the business sets clear expectations at the start of the application process and doesn't burn any bridges.

Here is my standard 'no' letter.

Dear _____,

Thank you for your application and interview for the position of sales representative. We were fortunate to receive over 70 applications. In this instance you have been unsuccessful. I wish you all the best in the future and hope you find a position to suit your many talents.

Warm regards,

First contact

Many organisations spend a lot of time and money attracting and signing up candidates, yet often they have little focus on what happens next. The Highfliers system, however, doesn't stop when someone signs an employment contract. The next step, day 1, which I call 'first contact', is also a key part of an effective hiring process. Do it well and the new person commits to becoming a long-term employee. Do it badly and they will kick themselves for having made the wrong decision and more than likely turn over.

Why do I say this? Because many employers forget that the first day on a job is one of the most significant events in a person's life. They're excited about getting the position but also feel anxious about whether they've made the right choice. Many HR books and websites focus only on training needs for this day, which sends the wrong message to employers. This day is not about the organisation's requirements; it's all about the recruit's. They need to feel inspired and valued and receive such a great first impression that they'll rave about the company to their friends and family when they go home that night.

Here's what it takes:

- A warm welcome from the team with whom the person will be working, with dedicated time for social interaction such as a pre-work get-together, a welcome cake at morning tea time or something similar.

- A seat, a desk, a computer and a password.

- A welcome card and present.

- An initial briefing to give an overview of the business, address practical concerns (such as how wages are paid) and answer any questions they may have.

- A welcome pack containing practical details such as wages, uniforms or business card ordering.

- A hello from the organisation's leader or senior executives. I always roam around with my new people and get as many top dogs as possible to shake their hand.

- A buddy or mentor who can help answer their general questions.

These all sound simple, yet they're still rare in many organisations. I'll never forget the senior executive I met who'd been working in a company for four weeks and still didn't have a computer or internet password. His new organisation had paid a recruitment agency a 30 000-dollar success fee to hire him, but because of their lack of follow-through, he left in less than three months.

I've seen companies start employees when their managers are on holidays and ones who put people in front of computers, with minimal human interaction, for their first week. The outcome is always predictable. These recruits leave as soon as they've sourced a more empathetic employer. The saddest part is that many organisations don't even know this is happening because they don't keep data on their recruits. When American mega-retailer Walmart began measuring their new person turnover they were shocked to find that of the staff that were leaving, 67 per cent went in the first 90 days.

Employing the best people

The process for making an objective decision and employing a great recruit is summarised in figure 6.3.

Figure 6.3: the process of employing a great recruit

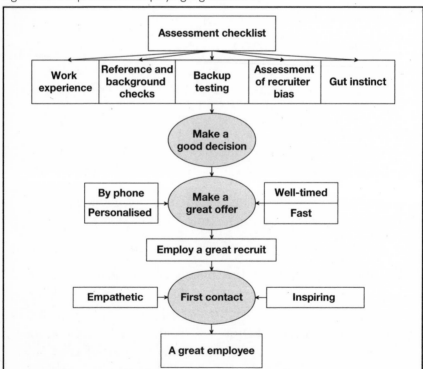

However, hiring a great employee is not just about making a great choice or putting together a brilliant offer. It's the natural culmination of the first six steps of the Highfliers 7-step System. Hence it follows that people with a holistic approach to hiring—who implement, analyse and improve every stage of their process—are those most likely to achieve recruitment success. As John Paul Getty, the rich American industrialist, said, 'The employer generally gets the employees he deserves'. In practice, I've found this to be true every time.

Engagement

Use the following questions to assess how your organisation could improve its process of choosing and engaging great people.

→ How do we make our recruitment decisions? Do we have an objective process for this?

→ Do we reference check to compare the interviewee's answers with those of the referee?

→ Do we use backup tests such as psychometric or skills tests only as adjuncts?

→ Do we use work experience to increase our new-recruit success rate?

→ What are our recruiter's biases?

→ What could we do to personalise our job offers?

→ How can we make our job offers faster and more inspiring?

→ How can we give new recruits a great 'first contact' warm welcome?

→ How can we make our rejection letters more empathetic?

→ On a scale of 1 to 10 with 1 being the worst and 10 being the best, how would we rate our company's induction process in the following areas?

  o Our new recruits feel valued.

  o Our new recruits feel inspired.

  o Our new recruits have somewhere to go to with their queries and concerns.

→ What tools can we develop to make someone's first day of work an excellent experience?

CHAPTER 7

Retaining: keeping your highfliers

In my 50-odd years in the business world, I have noticed that those people who were able to expand their enterprises... understood that the bottom line is ultimately the result of human endeavour.

Don Argus, ex-Chairman of global mining company BHP Billiton

The sun was shining outside, yet I felt sick in my stomach. My colleague Gary 'Boxer' Hogan and I were scanning the profit and loss figures for Flight Centre's UK start-up operation and all we could see was red ink. After working 18-hour days, finding and fitting out stores, recruiting, training and managing staff, negotiating deals with airlines and tour companies, and constantly improving all of our operational and IT systems, we'd opened 10 shops in 18 months. Yet while some stores were making profits, more were making losses and we didn't know why. We sat there all afternoon crunching figures and trying to find some answers for the company's board members, who were arriving the following week. At 8 pm we gave up and left, aware that our jobs were on the line and that the whole venture was in danger of being shut down.

When Boxer rang me the next morning however, he was euphoric. He'd discovered that every person who'd been employed for 12 months or longer *was* making an individual profit for the company. We *were* successful. It just wasn't obvious because every time we opened another shop we diluted our figures as the ratio of new-to-'old' staff stayed high. By these calculations, if we kept expanding at our current rate and retained the bulk of our people, within a year we'd have more experienced than new employees. The operation would then reach a tipping point and become profitable.

'That's brilliant!' I shouted down the phone at this revelation.

'Well at least it's a theory,' he replied dryly.

A week later we presented our findings to the board and were fortunate that they believed us.

The company's UK growth, profitability and very survival then became reliant on one dominant strategy: staff retention. We'd got great people on board using many Highfliers techniques, but now it was essential to keep them. When Barbara, a brilliant young recruit, quit the day after the board left, I felt it as a physical blow. We redoubled our efforts and finally made an inaugural profit 12 months later. The theory was proven. The enterprise never went backwards from there. The UK is now Flight Centre's most profitable operation after Australia and in June 2012 had 215 businesses and a turnover of $1.2 billion. Had we not realised the tangible value of keeping our people, the outcome would have been very different.

This experience taught me that:

> *Recruiting good people without a system for* keeping *them is like pouring liquid gold into a bathtub and not putting in the plug.*

It's simply a waste of everyone's valuable time and energy.

The big 'wham' strategies for staff retention

So what are the key strategies for keeping good people? This question is critical because the most effective techniques are not always the obvious ones. Take one of my clients, who seemed to offer it all. They paid their employees a high incentivised salary, gave them a day off on their birthdays, built an in-house coffee shop with their own barista, subsidised lunches, provided free fruit baskets and took the managers away on an all-expenses paid conference once a year. Yet their staff turnover rate was a staggering 64 per cent. Their list of seemingly impressive initiatives was longer than most Chinese restaurant menus, but they had zero focus. They threw perks at their employees like lollies to children, but used very few of the real techniques that truly keep people around.

It's the 80/20 rule: 20 per cent of strategies have a greater impact on staff turnover than all of the other 80 per cent put together. If you look at figure 7.1 you'll see my list of big 'wham' items—the practices built on a foundation of effective recruitment—which have been proven both through my direct experience and empirical research to lead to the most outstanding staff retention success.

Figure 7.1: effective retention

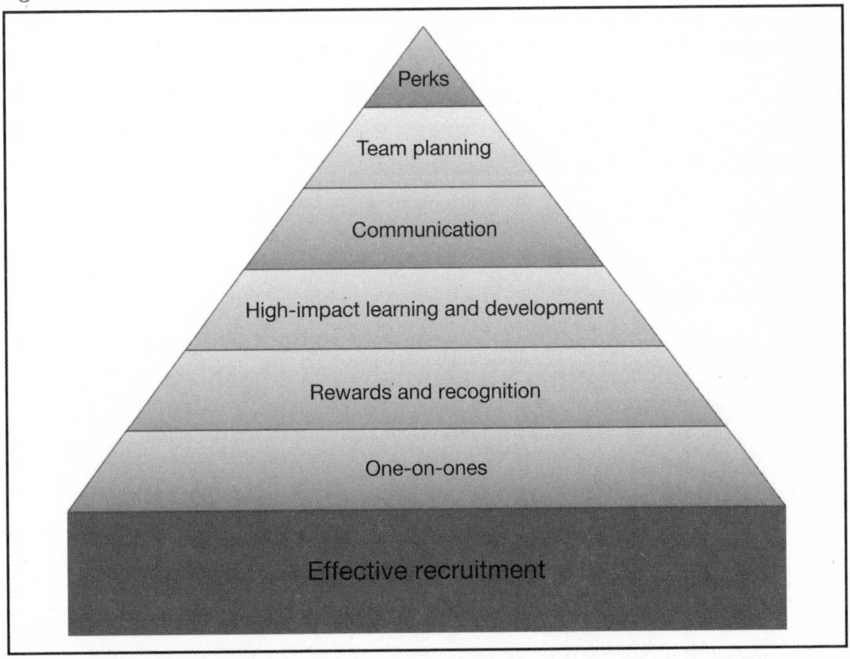

These six factors look deceptively simple but their impact on an organisation is transforming.

One-on-ones—the pulse of an organisation

As a new retail manager, my first gig was in one of the worst performing stores in the Flight Centre group. It hadn't made a profit for five years, it was in the sticks (an hour out of the city) and three of the five staff were on the brink of leaving at the first available opportunity. My peers took great delight in telling me I'd been handed a poisoned chalice, one the company had been trying to offload onto some sucker for months. When I asked my boss for guidance, his helpful reply was 'just sort it', and then he stopped taking my calls.

With no real idea where to start, I sat down with each employee to find out what they saw as the challenges within the business and for themselves. These initial get-togethers took a couple of hours, as I got to know each person and they aired all their bottled-up thoughts (and believe me, they had quite a few). Yet once I'd done these 'one-on-ones' I knew exactly what to do. I asked the team to come up with ideas for improvement and a personal action plan, and we implemented them step by step. Three months later, with everyone still on board, the shop made its first monthly profit in five years. It never went into the red again and my one-on-ones dropped back to a pleasant half-hour each over coffee once I'd cleared out the backlog of problems.

Of all the management strategies I've ever seen or used, the monthly one-on-one system—during which a manager takes time out to have a productive, reflective discussion with each employee and create an action plan—is a standout. It's also the single greatest weapon for winning the staff retention battle. I say this because the most important relationship in an organisation is the one that exists between an employee and their immediate supervisor. If this connection flourishes, so does the business. This is what one-on-ones cultivate. They're a superb tool for managers to build strong bonds with team members, which is why learning how to do them well is the best leadership training ever.

They also do the following:

- *Identify common problems to be acted on.* One-on-ones enable leaders to gauge the pulse of an organisation and find out what's *really* going on. If one person says the new IT system is twice as cumbersome as the old one, or that customer enquiries have plummeted because of poor ads, then that individual may just be a whinger or externalising to compensate for their own lack of results. But if everyone is highlighting the same issue, then it's something real that needs to be addressed. For instance, our UK employees kept telling us that our charter flight booking system was ineffective. (They actually used a very effective four-letter word to describe how ineffective it was!) This became a key organisational system change. By keeping everyone updated monthly on what was happening to source and build a new system over the next 12 months, we didn't lose anyone over this issue. It's a win-win. The organisation identifies and solves common problems and employees, empowered when their voices are heard and acted on, are far less likely to leave.

- *Inspire with the big picture.* It's so easy for employees and managers alike to get caught up in day-to-day activities, focusing only on perspiration, not inspiration. Yet employees want to work for organisations that have a clear direction and purpose which engages and enthuses them. One-on-ones create a dedicated time for telling the business story, including people in the vision and sharing with them how their actions contribute to moving the business forward. If people feel like and are genuinely part of something bigger than themselves, they become more motivated and productive, and are less likely to leave.

- *Help people develop, both personally and professionally.* By flipping from the conventional appraisal attitude of telling or disciplining to a more open approach of listening, exploring and resolving, one-on-ones become a power tool for improving people's skills and capabilities. The added bonus is that there's rarely any need to sack anyone. When people face up squarely to poor performance each month through the non-achievement of their own action plans, they either improve, or they leave of their own volition. This cuts the need for HR mediators too, because when people are talking to each other regularly, they don't need a middle person to sort out problems.

Ironically, all of the above occur naturally in a start-up business. When an enterprise consists of a small, agile team, communication and trust are a natural part of the process. Everyone knows what's going on, they're an integral part of the big picture, they can make change and, through the chief's hands-on involvement, give and receive regular meaningful feedback.

Yet as an organisation grows, so does the need for a formalised one-on-one system, at every level. The head of finance needs to do them with their team, the IT chief with their technicians, the regional manager with their business leaders, the CEO with the executive team and so on. It's only in this way that larger organisations can replicate the responsiveness of smaller enterprises.

A study by Bersin & Associates[18] found that actionable development plans alone result in twice the revenue per employee and a 27 per cent lower staff turnover rate. Yet most businesses still don't use them, preferring to stick with their conventional unproductive annual appraisal system. As the HR head of software company Atlassian, Joris Luijke found when he analysed their twice-yearly performance appraisals that '…the model did exactly the opposite to what we wanted to accomplish. Instead of an inspiring discussion about how to enhance people's performance, the two reviews caused disruptions, anxiety and de-motivated team members and managers'.[19] The company ripped their original model apart and implemented monthly check-ins. This required some restructuring as some teams were too big for one manager to do effectively. The results were worth the effort, however. The organisation has since won numerous 'best employer' awards; both independent and internal staff engagement surveys show extraordinary high engagement scores of 87 per cent and 83 per cent respectively; and the company has found the smaller, more flexible teams they created have been a boon to their bottom line.

One of the main reasons employers give for not doing regular one-on-ones is lack of time. They see them as simply more meetings—unproductive 'out-of-office' sessions. Yet because they've never done them, they've never witnessed the awesome power that they unleash. Imagine a sportsperson seeing their coach only once or twice a year. It just wouldn't happen. The same applies in business. Doing one-on-ones regularly actually saves time by reducing office conflict and stress, defusing complaints, expediting solutions and improving performance. Workers become happier, customers better served, and the leader can focus on business planning, strategising and celebrating, rather than continually recruiting and cracking the whip. It's a far more satisfying experience for everyone.

Inspiring, effective one-on-ones

As with any system, reading about it is one thing; implementing it correctly is another. The basic ingredients for conducting an inspiring and effective one-on-one are:

- preparation
- leading the one-on-one process
- following up.

Preparation

Good one-on-ones require preparation. It's essential to gather objective evidence throughout the month that can be used to celebrate achievement or as an example of poor performance. Even reading last month's action plan can help clarify thinking. Another great guide is to ask employees for their agenda topics or to fill out a progress report with examples of what they feel they've done well for the month and what they think they can improve on, with actionable suggestions. This kind of preparation creates far better outcomes than if a leader simply tries to wing it.

Leading the one-on-one process

Some of the most transformational ideas have come from people on the frontline, not from the suits in the boardroom. A one-on-one, then, is to be viewed as a voyage of discovery. Attitude is everything. If a leader embarks on it from the standpoint that they really want to listen and find out how best they can encourage this employee—and they back this up with a positive, honest, objective approach—then the interaction will be highly successful.

4-step process for a one-on-one

Here's an effective 4-step process for achieving the best possible results during a one-on-one.

1 *Ask for the employee's perspective.* By listening first, rather than speaking, and by asking probing questions, it's amazing how often assumptions about people's underlying beliefs and actions are proven wrong. As trust builds and the critical manager–employee relationship flourishes, people will often share more relevant information that fast tracks solutions.

2 *Give the organisation's perspective.* Give staff feedback on the points they've raised from the business perspective using objective examples and explaining the impact, good or bad. This is where a lot of issues are resolved because if people understand the reasons behind seemingly arbitrary decisions, or learn that their particular bugbear hasn't been acted on because it isn't shared by the majority, they're more content with organisational outcomes.

3 *Discuss performance.* Acknowledge and express appreciation for good performance and/or discuss reasons and consequences for poor performance and brainstorm solutions with them.

4 *Create an action plan.* Create a personalised action plan from the points raised. In the case of the leader it may be chasing up an employee's overtime pay or raising a specific issue in the next management meeting. The employee creates a goal and strategy for next month (it's much more powerful if they come up with this themselves) that relates to ways they can improve performance, skills, behaviour or actions. Both parties diarise what needs to be done and the plan is filed for review the following month.

Following up

An effective one-on-one doesn't finish at the door of the coffee shop. The most important—yet often most neglected—factor in achieving success lies in the follow up. Sometimes it's a quick fix such as amending an office policy, booking a training course or simply asking someone how their plan is tracking. If it's an organisational concern it becomes a priority for the manager to send this information up the line and keep everyone posted on progress.

My final caveat on one-on-ones is that if an organisation introduces them and then does nothing about the major common issues aired across the board, the effect on retention will be disastrous. People are intelligent and expect to be treated that way. There's nothing guaranteed to incense them more than words that don't align with actions, and good employees (and their leaders) will always bail out when the company doesn't follow through on its promises.

Reward and recognition

I was once invited to a client conference that also doubled as an annual staff awards night. It was a gala affair: black tie, five-star dining and great entertainment preceding an Academy Awards-style presentation. Yet I was confused to find that the prevailing mood afterwards was one of deep resentment. When I asked an attendee about this he explained to me, 'None of these awards are fair. Brian (who got the Managing Director's Award) gets a prize every year even though his area is 40 per cent down in profit and most of his staff think he is useless'.

Another chimed in bitterly, 'And Sarah, who got the "Most Organised" Award, is the boss's personal assistant. You can be the most outstanding employee in the company but unless you're one of his favourites you'll never get a look-in'.

This organisation had spent thousands flying their people overseas, all with good intent, but they'd sabotaged any potential return on this investment through their unconsciously subjective process.

This was the first time I'd seen a rewards and recognition system that was highly generous, yet actively demotivated people. It wouldn't be the last. In my career I've seen so many bad applications that I'm beginning to think they're the norm rather than the exception. Yet, as a 2012 Globoforce survey[20] of US workers found, 55 per cent of employees said they would leave their organisation for one that recognised their efforts and 47 per cent gave that as the main reason for leaving their last job. Turn this around and there's a serious prize on offer for companies who can get this right.

Key components of a successful rewards and recognition system

Like many things in this book, it's not the complexity of these systems that makes them effective, it's the simplicity. I've now implemented successful schemes in a diverse range of industries and organisations such as retailers, hotels and even a cattle station. The key components of my step-by-step approach for ensuring success is summed up in figure 7.2.

Figure 7.2: key steps for rewarding and recognising people effectively

This circular approach aligns all the people practices with the desired business outcomes so it increases operational excellence as well as retention.

Key Performance Indicators (KPIs)

KPIs are the foundation stones of any effective rewards and recognition system because they enable an organisation to *objectively* measure and compare output. They also promote autonomy because employees can track and improve their own performance. The results speak for themselves. High achievers stand out like shining lights and can be rewarded and recognised (and are less likely to leave) and those on the other end of the scale will be just as obvious. Without the need for constant management observation, roles can also be more flexible and this in turn attracts more highfliers to the organisation.

It's all about the implementation. Effective KPIs that are embraced by employees produce MAGIC results.

MAGIC

Here's the basis for MAGIC KPIs.

Monthly

Effective KPIs can be tracked and reported monthly, so they have continuous 'real time' relevance to the employee.

Achievable

KPIs are realistically attainable yet still act as real motivation. Too often companies put in place impossible stretch targets and of course are then happy to pay bonuses for superhuman performances.

Goal-oriented

KPIs are aligned with the desired business outcomes of the individual's actual job role and drive real business achievement.

Individual results

KPIs are most productive if a person feels they are in direct control of the outcome, so they work best when they're based on the individual's performance, and not on team results.

Clear and simple

KPIs are objective—not subjective—and simple enough that employees are able to calculate them in their heads and don't require a degree in complex logistics to work them out.

MAGIC KPIs work best if there are only one to three per job role as any more dilutes people's focus and consequently the outcomes.

Setting KPIs to achieve the best outcomes

The right KPIs invigorate employees. They can see how they measure up against others in similar roles, and this is a powerful motivator for good performers. When I was a travel agent, a travel insurance company introduced a ranking table that, for the first time, showed where every consultant ranked against others in the company based on the dollar value of policies sold. I was shocked to find out that I was only in sixty-fourth place. The following month, I sold more insurance than I'd ever sold before and came in at number 28. Others did the same. With everyone working to improve rankings by honing up on product knowledge and sales prompts, the insurance company *doubled* its sales in a single month (and the employees earned a lot more money in commission too).

This is the true power of KPIs. Like a magnifying glass that focuses sunlight onto one point to create a powerful flame, KPIs produce excellence by directing people's attention onto achievement, not just 'doing'. This is critical for retention. Employees who are fully engaged in what they're doing and can see exciting, measurable improvements don't spend their time browsing job-search sites.

Yet this only happens with a well-thought-out system. KPIs are usually obvious for positions where the outcomes are very measurable, such as sales-based roles. For other positions in which measurement is not obvious, such as marketing managers, maintenance people or IT Help Desk personnel, many employers simply don't know where to begin.

Table 7.1 consists of a set of questions that will help guide you through the process of defining effective KPIs.

I also always ask existing employees for their input. Often they will have good ideas on how their role can be measured and through this involvement they also take ownership of the outcome.

Table 7.1: designing effective KPIs and incentives for any role

Question	Example	Comment
1 Why does this area of the business exist? What are the main one or two outcomes that it contributes to the organisation?	The purpose of the recruitment area is to enable an organisation to employ and retain the best people for the business.	Focus on the ultimate raison d'être of the area, not necessarily the specific core skill.
2 How can you objectively measure this?	Quality: The number of new recruits each month that achieve performance targets in their fourth month of employment Quantity: The number of vacancies filled, less turnover	Note that if you can't come up with a way to objectively measure a business outcome, then it cannot be used for the purpose of KPIs.
3 What systems do you need to create?	Quality: A standard agreed method on the performance targets indicative of a good recruit Quantity: A standard agreed method to measure staff turnover every month Support systems: A monthly KPI form for employees to tally up their overall progress on each measurement and a whole department spreadsheet that collates all the individual results	Often some new systems may need to be created before KPIs can be implemented. This valuable information can then be used as an analysis and reporting tool for executive discussion and the objective data helps everyone make more informed decisions

(continued)

Table 7.1: designing effective KPIs and incentives for any role (cont'd)

Question	Example	Comment
4 How can you use KPIs to monetarily incentivise people (if required)? a) First work out the total salary for this position and how much you want the incentives to be	Let's say the average market salary for a recruiter is $70 000 so an organisation may decide on a base salary of $50 000 plus $20 000 in incentives: $10 000 for achieving quantity outcomes and $10 000 for achieving the quality incomes. This equates to $833 per month in each category	The $ amount of the incentives should be enough to act as real motivation, be realistically achievable and offer people the ability to excel beyond the average earnings
b) Now determine the current average achievement in each category	Quality: The number of vacancies filled, less turnover; currently averages 8 each month per recruiter Quantity: The current average number of new recruits reaching performance targets at the 4-month mark is 6 per recruiter	If this criteria has never been measured before this will involve a month or two of assessment
c) Now divide the $ incentive amounts by these averages to get real incentive payment figures	Quantity: The number of vacancies filled, less turnover: $833 ÷ 8 = approx. $100 A recruiter earns $100 for every vacancy filled each month, less $100 for every new recruit that leaves the business that month, having stayed less than 3 months with the organisation. Quality: The number of new recruits each month that achieve performance targets: $833 ÷ 6 = approx. $140 A recruiter earns $140 for every new recruit they have employed who in their 16th to 20th weeks achieves or exceeds all of their set performance targets.	Make sure you define each aspect of the incentive in a detailed system. For instance, in this example is it 3 calendar months or 90 days? Note that because the incentives are aligned with the business outcomes, the more a recruiter achieves, the more profit is created for the business so there is no need to cap them.

Inspirational incentives

My friend Mary was working for a swanky global retail brand that everyone knows. They had amazing business systems: automated supply ordering and a sales IT system that broke targets and reporting down into minutes and hours. But when I asked her how much she was earning on each sale she didn't know.

'I get some form of bonus,' she said. 'I'm just not sure what it is.'

I followed her up three months later to find out she'd just become one of the top rookie salespeople nationwide and had received her first bonus...it was a 50-dollar gift voucher to be used in-store (on marked-up products that started at $100!). She was less than impressed and told me she was actively job hunting.

This is a great example of how poor incentives lead to a self-defeating cycle. The company only paid trifling bonuses on huge targets and in fact was struggling to make profits, yet if they had rewarded their staff on every sale, they would have increased their sales and profits and reduced staff turnover as well.

Like designing a good recruitment ad, creating a sound foundation of KPIs and incentive schemes takes time and thought. Yet these incentives act like kerosene on the KPI flame. When employees who were initially resistant to them (and rightly so if the scheme is a shocker) discover they're rewarded for the effort they put in, not just for turning up, enthusiasm skyrockets and achievement records are broken. People love the fact that they can boost their own wages because with incentives aligned to business outcomes there's no need for them to ever be capped. These new raving fans then attract more highfliers to the organisation, creating a continuous circle of improvement.

With so many obvious advantages, why then are the bulk of companies still resistant to the very idea of incentives? I understand that the ability to implement them is constrained in some organisations — such as public service departments; however, other businesses are missing out on an extraordinary opportunity to transform their results. A study undertaken by The Incentive Research Foundation found that properly structured incentive programs that run for a year or longer produce an average 44 per cent performance increase and enable employers to attract and retain higher quality workers than organisations with no incentive program.[21] This was backed up by renowned business analyst and author Robert Gottliebsen, who rated Flight Centre's incentive scheme as one of the best in his book *10 Best and 10 Worst Decisions of Australian CEOs*. He said, 'These sorts of shops and businesses earn substantially more profits than those with traditional staff arrangements. It is stunning that other major retailers have not followed their lead'.[22]

Public recognition

I first started at Flight Centre two months before the annual awards night and I was amazed at how excited everyone was as they competed to earn the top spots. One person was offered a free 10-day Maldives tour but turned it down as she was in the lead for the Consultant of the Year Award. Another brought her sleeping bag to work and set it up in the back office so she could process more enquiries overnight. Many of these front-runners made fivefold the sales they would in ordinary months.

At the awards night the reasons became clear. The winners were feted on stage like superstars. At the climax of the night, when the Consultant of the Year was announced and showered with streamers, the emotion of the audience was electrifying. At the after-party a colleague said to me, 'That's going to be me up on stage next year'...and it was.

As business author Michael LeBoeuf says in his book *How to Motivate People*, 'While money can be a very powerful incentive, recognition can be even more powerful...it is amazing how hard people will work when the payoff is feeling appreciated and important'.[23]

Awards nights, however, are not enough to sustain this buzz. As Globoforce found in their 2012 Moodtracker Survey, 'the more frequently people are recognised, the more engaged and satisfied employees they become'. Here are a few other ways people can be recognised to keep the momentum going all year:

- The CEO can name and congratulate top performers in their newsletter every month. This is an organisation's most powerful recognition tool.

- Highfliers can be ranked on an intranet site or have their names placed on a public 'Hall of Fame' board at head office.

- Local awards nights (we called ours Buzz Nights) can be held quarterly to recognise achievers and to hand out certificates and small prizes such as book vouchers.

- Outstanding recruits can star on the company's careers website.

- Outstanding novices who demonstrate leadership potential can be placed on a fast-track future leaders program.

- Experts can be recognised as specialists or mentors in their field or be invited to participate in the development of new initiatives for their area.

Once an organisation is tuned in to recognising its people, it's amazing how many opportunities can be identified. The results speak for themselves. Delta Airlines reported a 564 per cent return on investment (ROI) on its rewards and recognition program.[24] The Avis Budget Group designed a recognition program and put it online to make it simple to nominate, approve and distribute awards. They experienced a 3.8 per cent drop in staff turnover at a time when the industry average was increasing and, at $3 million per percentage point, that equated to a massive $11.4 million profit bounce.[25] Sutherland Global Services, a 24-site, 24 000-employee global service company, says the money they put into recognition earns a 20-times return and is the company's best investment. Senior Vice President Tom Steuwe's only grievance? 'I am kicking myself for not having done this five or six years ago.'[26]

High-impact learning and development (L&D)

The first time I realised that the way I thought about learning and development was very different from everyone else's way was during a conversation I had with a neighbour some years ago. I told Mick, the owner of a large maintenance business, that I'd spent the morning running a sales training seminar.

'Feeding the chooks you mean,' he said. Seeing my confused expression he explained, 'You know, training. Useless exercise. Never makes much difference. Big waste of money but as employers we have to be seen to be going through the motions to keep our people happy'.

I've implemented training programs with extraordinary results — businesses doubling their profit figures, a bike chain increasing its sales by 20 per cent in one week, the worst performing offices in a region becoming the best — so I know that quality training can be instrumental in developing people and achieving corporate goals. Yet I was to learn over time that Mick's opinion of corporate L&D was shared by many. I also came to accept that it was often entirely justified.

This depressing discovery came about as a result of a consulting project I undertook to implement a suite of training products for a 500-employee company. I started off with high hopes, energised by the thought of the many wonderful products awaiting me. After reviewing hundreds of local, national and global courses, however, I uncovered a very different reality. Yes, there were some excellent providers out there, but they were swamped by the sheer mass of firms peddling mediocrity: high-profile universities whose 'world class' product consisted of monotonous two-hour videos of a person talking into a camera; online companies whose sub-standard modules were more e-Information than eLearning; and external 'experts' who had simply hung up their shingle or bought into a coaching/training franchise that gave them support tools and formats but couldn't substitute for their lack of real business success.

It's these kinds of defective offerings that have distorted the whole discussion about L&D and convinced a generation of CEOs that it's futile to expend much energy in this area. I now understand why one frustrated head said to me in an initial consult, 'We've spent $5 million on training over the past five years and we've got f★★★-all to show for it!'

Call me old-fashioned, but if I pay good money to take my people out of the business and send them on a sales course, I want to know that they will sell more afterwards. It's this kind of transference of real skills from the classroom to the workplace that every business leader craves. It's where L&D delivers the bang for the buck, the fundamental reason for its existence. It's also what highfliers now expect from an organisation: high-impact training that develops them personally and professionally, unlike the 'sheep-dip' training of old. For those with increased retention in their sights, it's an essential part of the package in the twenty-first century workforce.

The characteristics of high-impact L&D

The characteristics that underpin high-impact L&D are as follows:

- *Quality not quantity.* As an HR leader I once asked our regional managers what they would like included in the induction process. Once I'd collated all their responses I had enough information to keep a person busy for about two years. In practice I've found that just a few inspirational sessions have greater impact than hundreds of mediocre ones.

- *Short and sharp.* I've never had the budget luxury of being able to send my employees out of the office for days at a time so I've always looked for short, sharp or bite-sized programs, a day or less, that really inspire people—ones that I could be certain would deliver that holy grail of transference from the classroom to the workplace. Unfortunately trainers are actually incentivised to drag programs out as they get paid more for longer sessions.

- *Fun and engaging.* Every successful L&D course has an engaging element of fun, interactivity or 'theatre'. Anthony Robbins, with his 'walking across hot coals' exercise, which shows people they can achieve things they thought were impossible, is a master of the 'show'. Yet participants tell me that his content is also transformative. It's this winning combination of the two — process and content — that makes people remember, learn and apply new actions. In contrast, many courses have good content but sitting through them is like being fed horse tranquilisers. I'll never forget a three-day strategic planning course — for which I paid $2500 — where the facilitator gave us a folder and then read through it for the duration of the course. Without any entertainment or interactivity (process), I didn't retain a thing.

- *Relevance.* This should be obvious, but in practice it's not. One of my clients who ran a sales business had hundreds of L&D modules but not one sales course. His new recruits learned how to sit in a chair to avoid back strain, what to do if they were bullied or sexually harassed, and absolutely every facet of how to use the IT system in over 30 separate courses. Yet they weren't taught how to handle customers and convert their enquiries into sales. I felt sorry for these novices, especially as all the business leaders kept complaining to me about the time it took employees to get up to speed and how they seemed incapable of reaching their targets. On the positive side, they did sit very upright in their chairs.

Building an inspirational L&D system

With these characteristics in mind, how does an organisation build or transform an existing area into a high-impact L&D system? My step-by-step approach is summarised in figure 7.3.

Figure 7.3: steps for building a high-impact L&D system

Effective L&D infrastructure → A core business curriculum → Inspirational L&D activities → Reinforce, measure and improve

Once again the focus is on simplicity and effectiveness.

Effective L&D infrastructure: the bones of great L&D

There are some basic ingredients required for an L&D system to be effective. Just like great recruitment, these are:

- a positive corporate attitude

- a highflying leader with the ear of the CEO

- an L&D team focused on L&D, not stacked up with policy production, quality certification or any other types of non-L&D administrative activities.

Yet the biggest mistake I see repeated time and again is when L&D staff, often juniors with limited expertise in the subject area, create training modules. This is sheer madness. With little or no input from relevant business leaders or experts in the role, the programs developed are generally useless to frontline staff and are often ignored. The L&D team's response? They make the ineffectual course compulsory and put in a system of policing measures to make sure everyone does it.

This is what I call 'training for the sake of training'—work undertaken to justify people's employment in an L&D area, rather than any initiatives that make a real difference. It's letting the tail wag the dog. Yes, L&D is that area's responsibility, but they should be like project managers, coordinating other experts and achievers both internally and externally to produce or provide modules with real business outcomes. The first questions for any new training course, then, should be:

> 'Who is the key stakeholder?'
> 'Who is the end user?'

And the ultimate litmus test is:

> 'Are they prepared to pay for it?'

Like the development of a new IT product, the best results occur when the organisation's business leaders take ownership of cost and outcomes.

The core business curriculum

When I started up Flight Centre's first training and recruitment centre, which operated as a real store, I'd always thought product knowledge would give new people the biggest lift. The data quickly showed the reverse was true. The best results were achieved when we taught recruits how to develop good relationships with people. By coaching them on how to build rapport, ask questions and identify real needs, we were amazed to find our newbies in their first month doubled the number of customer enquiries they turned into sales, compared to our previous measurements.

As well as the core skills people require just to do their job I believe there's a core business curriculum relevant across all organisations and industries that really drive outcomes. This core curriculum consists of:

- sales
- business, team and personal planning
- leadership
- relationship building
- customer service.

Less is more. Any company that sources even two great modules in each of these core areas, and measures and improves them for continuous effectiveness, will cover off on more things that have been proven to drive business success than in the hundreds of courses that pass as the norm in many organisations or by learning providers. Notice that these are mainly people-based processes. The underlying principle here is that in our social lives we can choose who we build relationships with. In our work lives we can't. We need to get along with everyone to achieve success.

The eLearning question

At one HR conference I attended everyone I spoke to was obsessed with eLearning. This is understandable. eLearning has a lot of obvious benefits. For example, it is:

- much cheaper than classroom training when transport and instructor costs are taken into account

- easy to deliver across large geographical distances and to a high volume of people

- consistent, unlike classroom training, which is presenter dependent

- great for just-in-time information that needs to be communicated quickly.

I was intrigued then, when one of my clients, who had adopted eLearning with such passion that they'd won numerous international awards for their online modules, recruited five full-time in-house trainers. This was at considerable expense so I asked the L&D manager for the reasons behind his decision.

He didn't think about his answer for long. 'We measured the overall effect on our bottom line,' he said, 'and our suite of "world class" eLearning workshops made absolutely no difference at all'.

I was amazed! I'd finally met one of the reported 3 per cent of respondents who actually measure the business results of training programs.[27]

Herein lies the challenge for all online learning. I'm no technology expert, but I do understand business outcomes. Online formats are a good option if someone needs to tick a box to get certification for serving alcohol and food, or requires a safety licence for a building site, or if an organisation wants to ensure that all its staff have read its sexual harassment policy. Yet this is not learning. It meets a need and industries burgeon from the provision of these products.

When it comes to the core business skills that really drive success, such as sales and leadership, however, what I see is a lot of e-information and very little learning going on. Most courses simply don't translate into real world ability. Everyone gets excellent online test scores (some just by Googling answers) but the majority don't remember or can't apply this knowledge in any meaningful way in the field.

In some cases the poor quality of the offerings is to blame. Often providers have simply taken their classroom courses, converted them to PowerPoint and spruced them up with videos and quizzes. For the digital generation raised on touchscreens and high-impact game technology this is like stepping back in time.

Yet this is irrelevant to organisations mesmerised by the huge dollars they save by rolling out an online product previously performed classroom style. Many online training decisions are being driven entirely by these cost-savings or by the volume of modules delivered. However, just like the manager in the example above who realised he'd wasted his $5 million, these companies are still not asking the critical question: What is the real world outcome? The best training courses are often the most expensive because they work. They transform. If I had a choice of spending $10 000 on something that produced $50 000 versus $2000 on something that delivered me $1000, I know which way I'd go.

When an eLearning core business product can deliver even 75 per cent of the transference of skills of a great face-to-face module for 25 per cent of the cost, then it will be a true player in the market. To date, most have not been able to. I'm sure that at some stage someone will step into this space and spend the millions required, just as they do on movies and leisure games, to produce an experience that's truly suited to the twenty-first century. The Serious Games Institute in Europe is pushing this agenda and with the increasing clamour around learner experience, many companies are moving in this direction. The proof, as always, will be in the profit results.

Inspirational L&D activities

High-impact L&D is more than just training courses. I learned more about sales sitting beside a great salesperson for four hours than from participating in any module. Lots of activities have the potential to inspire people. It may be a thought-provoking conference seminar, a reference to a cutting-edge article recommended in the CEO's monthly newsletter, a great YouTube clip, a short Ted Talk or an innovative team bonding session. Look at the green tsunami Al Gore's documentary *An Inconvenient Truth* created. I've been inspired by speakers such as business guru Richard Branson, media personality and businesswomen's champion Ita Buttrose, and the first amputee to climb Mt Everest, Tom Whittaker. These kinds of personal stories and tales, hardships and woes can provide an electric charge, and the lessons learned often galvanise people to make real change in themselves and their own organisation.

Collaborative activities are also a great way to increase inspiration. As a new retail manager I didn't receive a scrap of leadership training, but I did meet up with all the managers in my area for lunch once a month. Every time I felt like quitting, I would get together with my peers and they'd encourage me, offer helpful solutions and entertain me with stories of their own stuff-ups. This was the number-one factor in retaining me at the time.

Reinforce, measure and improve

Many training programs fail because they exist in a bubble. A high-impact L&D program relies not only on its courses but also on the way this content is embedded into the learner's mind through regular reinforcement such as:

- quarterly booster courses to keep skills honed
- online training notes for easy reference following classroom sessions
- manager's coaching notes for every course, to enable effective manager follow-up
- mentoring/buddy programs
- online social forums where people can post queries and swap information.

Overall, though, it's an organisation's ability to shift L&D thinking from a quantity mindset to a high-impact mindset that will make the real difference to the outcomes. Rather than measuring number of modules completed or cost-savings, those that focus on transference in terms of profitability and productivity will be the ones that truly create a world-class product, world-class employees and world-class results.

Communication

I once consulted to a company that had just sacked its chief operating officer. The rumours surrounding this event were incredible: the company was going broke, so she'd left before this happened. No, no, the CEO had had a blazing row with her, or he'd had sex with her and sacked her. No, she was disgruntled because he wouldn't give her autonomy and half the executive team was about to follow her. And so on, and so on.

This discussion went on for weeks around the water cooler, distracting employees from their own purpose and affecting company results. It unsettled people and staff turnover increased. Because the organisation had not explained this major event, gossip and conjecture filled the gap. And believe me, the rumour-monger's theories were far worse than anything that happened in reality.

People like to be involved and feel like they are part of a cause rather than just working for someone else's. Sharing information demonstrates respect for people and indicates they're valued and appreciated. Yet many companies are still often reluctant to reveal challenges, strategies or actual profit figures. Let me spell this out:

> *The most successful companies I've worked with have always been the most transparent.*

In a study by Accountemps[28], inadequate communication was cited as the primary cause of poor morale and this was almost double any other single factor. My friend Kathleen summed it up to me after she quit her job in disgruntlement 'because none of us knew what was going on, we didn't feel any connection to what we were doing and we didn't feel any loyalty to the people we were working for'.

Often the problem occurs because companies who were great at connecting with their people when they were small, lost this ability as they grew larger. This is why it's necessary to formalise an approach to communication ensuring employees have regular access to accurate information, which then increases retention. Have a look at figure 7.4 for an example of a successful communication system of this type.

Figure 7.4: example of a communication system

1 Within each team

Daily: a team brief to swap information (5 to10 minutes) and a mini-planner

Weekly: a team business meeting to swap information, and to discuss strategy and track performance (1 hour)

Monthly:

- a team business meeting to discuss monthly results, work on next month's strategy and celebrate success (1 hour)

- a one-on-one between the manager and each individual in the team

Annually: a team planning meeting to create a one-page action plan for the next 12 months.

2 Across the organisation

Daily: an intranet forum for day-to-day information sharing and posting of questions

Monthly: a newsletter from the CEO with recognition of high achievers and information on the progress of the overall company

Quarterly: a 'buzz night' with dinner and drinks for all people in each region of the company to communicate group information, celebrate success, and reward and recognise people for demonstrated achievement in front of their peers

Bi-annually: a team leaders' conference to discuss long-term strategy and direction

Annually:

- a staff conference to augment learning and personal development and educate and inspire people in the company's ongoing strategies

- a ball or awards night to celebrate success and reward and recognise the company's top performers in front of their peers.

You'll notice from figure 7.4 that regular communication is a great vehicle for rewarding and recognising people as well.

Team planning

Legendary American baseballer Babe Ruth once said, 'The way a team plays as a whole determines its success. You may have the greatest bunch of individual stars in the world, but if they don't play together, the club won't be worth a dime'.

This appeared to be the case when a friend of mine, a regional retail manager, asked me for help. He wanted me to train the employees of two of his businesses, which were making far less profit than his other stores. They were all skilled people, but they just didn't appear capable of producing results. I agreed to help, not knowing that my answer would set off a chain of events that would consume the next two years of my life.

The leader wanted sales training, but after much research and thought I convinced him to let me run a team-planning workshop instead. Like Formula One drivers who pull in for a pit-stop during a Grand Prix race, my four-hour session would take the team out of the business to analyse their current state of repair, and then they could collaboratively work on a simple, one-page plan of practical solutions to their current business challenges. By doing this the aim was that everyone would take ownership and be highly motivated to make things happen on their return to the business.

This session worked really well on the day and I thought it would have an impact. The results, however, exceeded even my wildest expectations. Both stores doubled their profits in the following month. The company's CEO was so excited by these results that in the end we rolled the course out to 1500 of his teams around the globe. It was one of the most successful initiatives of my entire career. Many of the businesses demonstrated remarkable productivity improvements, and staff turnover plummeted as teams became more engaged.

Of course I'd heard all the old chestnuts: 'A champion team will always beat a team of champions', and 'The whole is greater than the sum of the parts'. I'd also seen a lot of evidence of this in sport. This was my first experience, however, of the underlying truth of team adages on a mass scale relating to business. It was also the first time I'd seen how important this type of team engagement was to retention. I know now that helping teams harness their own power and showing them how to use their individual strengths to improve performance and make coming to work each day an exciting adventure are vital to business success.

The reasons for this soon became clear.

- *A 'bottoms-up' rather than 'top-down' approach.* The conventional approach to business planning is that a manager attends an executive planning day, comes up with some company-devised strategies and then tries to get the team to run with them. The manager's challenge is akin to dragging dead horses across a desert. The staff have no buy-in because they've had no access to the rationale and reasons behind the strategies. They've just been told what to do or what's going to happen. But let me tell you a secret. People hate that! In contrast, the individuals who make up a team are like an incubator of ideas. Tapping into this creates energy and excitement that's impossible to replicate from the outside-in.

- *Everyone shares responsibility.* Each strategy on the plan is overseen by a different team member. Rather than one team leader trying to make eight things happen, eight team members are now responsible for just one technique — such as marketing, training or social events — and everyone takes responsibility for the outcomes. With eight people now rowing, the business powers ahead like never before. And as we all know, no-one wants to leave a winning team.

So what happened to my original client? In the end the company took the whole process in-house and annual team business plans became a standard part of their business model. After rolling it out, I spent some time with the CEO analysing the results to examine in more detail why they have such a powerful effect.

He had a simple explanation. 'Mandy, it almost doesn't matter what plan the team comes up with. As long as it's their plan then they're all making it happen.'

Big data mining

There was one other enormous benefit to the company of this team-planning process. Because every business was developing a plan, across the many hundreds of enterprises it was possible to gather common, meaningful information. It was big data mining at its best—the top challenges, the top training needs, the top marketing initiatives, the top desired improvements and so on. By consolidating all of these into a single report the organisation created a top-10 list for change driven from the floor, a valuable blueprint to act on and keep its good people.

Perks

Everybody loves to talk about perks and there are lots of articles and blogs devoted to the merits of one versus another. They are certainly attention–grabbers: the slippery slide between office floors; neck massages at the desk; the indoor climbing wall; the pet-friendly workplace.

Yes, perks make people feel valued and give them something to boast about to their friends. Yet I put them at the very tip of the retention pyramid because that's what they are: the icing on the cake. Too often I see organisations relying on perks as their central recruitment and retention strategy, but as a survey by Glassdoor[29] found, only one in five employees rated them as important in comparison to other retention mechanisms.

Perks are only useful, then, when they align with a company's attitude, values and strategies in regard to its people. Take SAS, the US software company that ranked as number one in the world for best workplaces in 2012.[30] Their philosophy is 'to value people above all else' and they have a real vision underlying their perks program: to relieve staff of causes of outside stress that may be distracting and enable them to better focus on their work.

Here are just a few examples of what they offer: child care centres, support for elder care, a recreation and fitness centre, retirement and healthcare services, car detailing, dry cleaning, nail and skin care salons, a lending library, a summer camp for children and even a tennis racquet restringing service. It sounds more like a resort than a workplace!

SAS CEO Jim Goodnight describes it as a triangle where happy employees make happy customers, which makes a happy company.[31] It's not surprising, then, that the company has the lowest staff turnover rate in the industry at 3.3 per cent (versus the industry norm of 22 per cent[32]), tens of thousands of applicants compete for its few hundred vacancies each year, and it's just delivered its thirty-seventh consecutive year of record profit and revenue earnings.

SAS is a large corporation. However, perks don't have to be expensive to be effective. A free breakfast once a month, casual dress days, games rooms and discounts with local businesses are all small budget items with impact.

Making perks staff-centric keeps them relevant and effective. For instance, there's no point putting digital games in your staffroom just because Google does it if your workforce is mainly mature women who hate arcade games. Taking the time to think of things that will really add value to people's lives, rather than taking a piecemeal approach, demonstrates tangible respect. To sum up, as long as they're aligned with company culture, 'perks works'.

Measure, measure, measure

Staff turnover is obviously the main KPI for retention, but one-on-ones and staff satisfaction surveys can also provide useful information as long as the surveys aren't overly complicated to justify expensive fees, of course. A few simple questions on each retention strategy or a single benchmarking score is more than adequate to determine improvement in specific areas and discourages subjective or anecdotal corporate decision-making.

Exit interviews: the canary in the coalmine

Exit interviews also provide an outstanding opportunity for business improvement and staff retention. These operate the same way as the canary down the coal mine by signalling when people processes are out of kilter. It may be that the salaries on offer are no longer competitive in the marketplace; that there are shortfalls in training; that there's a perceived lack of career opportunities or even that there's a rogue bully managing beautifully upwards to the chiefs but smothering their underlings. Whatever the case, this valuable feedback can identify endemic problems so they can be addressed before more people leave.

Yet like a great tool left to rust away in the garden shed, many businesses perform exit interviews and then do absolutely nothing with them. 'We do them because it's company policy', or 'The legal department told us to do them in case someone ever tries to sue for unfair dismissal,' are just two of the explanations I've heard for this kind of inactivity. My answer is that if you have to do them for a stupid reason, then use them for an effective one. Taking action on this feedback sends a powerful message to existing employees that there's a genuine desire for improvement and ensures more raving fans and boomerangs in the long term. Filing them just wastes everyone's time and money.

Return On Investment (ROI)

With all of these retention techniques the return on investment of each one is always much greater than the expense. Most are simple and cost-effective. They do take commitment and perseverance, however. Perhaps this was the reason for the results of the 2012 Gallup Poll of 142 countries, which found that only 13 per cent of people across the world were engaged at work.[33] This is about one in every eight. Even worse, 24 per cent were actively disengaged, consciously undermining both their co-workers' and the organisation's success.

What exists in these figures is a massive opportunity. Because most businesses are still so poor at engaging their people, it means those that get good at it will have a real edge over their competitors. With a proactive corporate attitude, an HR champion, an L&D project manager and a committed approach to objective step-by-step improvement of people systems, an organisation can secure the cream of the crop.

The silver bullet solution for retention

To finish, there's just one more thing I need to share about retention. Everybody wants a silver bullet solution, the one strategy they can use that will fix all their staff turnover woes and ensure their people never want to leave. The good news is ... I have one!

There's one single factor that's responsible for nearly 75 per cent of staff retention. It's one that's hardly ever mentioned in the retention section of HR books and rarely practised by organisations. It's one of the keys to all business success and the closest thing ever to a silver bullet solution and gives an organisation the best chance of keeping great people and transforming their business profits:

The best staff retention strategy ever is ... great recruitment!

Like a diver and their oxygen tank, recruitment and retention are inextricably linked. Employ the right people — ones who are a good fit for the role and the corporate culture — and they will want to stay. Employ the wrong people and even the most mind-blowing retention techniques will be ineffective. As detailed in chapter 3, a good recruitment system places people's wants at its centre, so by implementing my Highfliers 7-step System and addressing factors such as flexible workplaces, brightness of future, engaging job roles, and inspirational vision and values as part of the hiring process, an organisation is already winning the battle for talent.

Recruitment and retention. People and profits. They're so intertwined that you can't neglect one without impacting heavily on the other. Yet it's more than this. I think ex-Apple CEO Steve Jobs summed up my overall philosophy best when he said, 'All we are is our ideas, or people. That's what keeps us going to work in the morning, to hang around these great bright people. I've always thought that recruiting is the heart and soul of what we do'.[34]

Retention

To assess how well your organisation retains people, answer the following questions.

→ What is our current company retention percentage?

→ What would raising this mean to our business?

→ Do our managers currently do monthly one-on-ones?

→ How do we reward and recognise our people?

→ Do we have KPIs or other forms of objective measurement in place for every individual?

→ Do we incentivise our people on what they do?

→ Do we have monthly, quarterly and annual awards to recognise highfliers?

→ Does the CEO send out a monthly newsletter congratulating highfliers?

→ On a scale of 1 to 10 with 1 being the worst and 10 being the best, how would we rate our L&D in the following areas?

- o Transference
- o Quality
- o Fun and engaging
- o Relevance
- o Inspirational activities
- o Objective measurement
- o Continuous improvement

→ Do we have effective L&D infrastructure in place, including an L&D leader with the ear of the CEO, and are our business leaders involved in the development of our L&D courses?

→ Do we offer a few brilliant courses in the key subjects of the core business curriculum?

→ Do our teams create their own annual plan?

→ Do we have an effective communication system in place?

→ What perks do we offer our people? Are they staff-centric?

Conclusion

The knowing/doing challenge

So that's it. That's the whole Highfliers 7-step System and just about every single thing I know about recruitment and retention and how it relates to a company's growth and profits. Knowing something, however, is not enough. It's the doing that counts.

I learned this after working with a guy called Hugh who was always going out with gorgeous women. This puzzled me because Hugh was average looking and he didn't have a charismatic personality. One night, at a work function, I was seated beside him so I decided to ask the question.

'Hugh, how come I always see you going out with beautiful girls?'

He threw his head back and laughed. 'Mandy, that's simple,' he replied. 'I just ask every attractive woman I meet to go out with me.'

Because I love KPIs and measurement, I had to create a chart for this phenomenon:

Hugh's technique in action

	Strike rate	No. of attractive women met	No. of these women asked for a date	No. of attractive women dated
Hugh	10%	100	100	10
Better looking men	30%	100	3	0

Hugh was sensational at *doing*, at implementation, and his reward was synonymous with his efforts. My advice, then, for those CEOs who can't sleep at night because they're worried about finding and keeping key people is simple and to the point: just start! You too will get beautiful results.

Once you've begun attacking the challenge head-on, there are a couple of other pitfalls to watch out for too. People often want to cherry-pick just a few elements of the Highfliers 7-step System but still hang on to some of their more conventional practices. One company I worked with changed to benefit-led ads but kept its mediocre recruiters. Another started screening people for attitude, but never sped up its hiring process. Any good innovation is a step forward but by not improving practices in a consistent systematic manner, success will be limited.

Part of the difficulty here is that after 100 years of HR stagnation, bureaucratisation and overdeveloped systems, simple can be harder than complex. Employers are often so conditioned to thinking they need massive, expensive initiatives to make real change that they discount or ignore all the easy things, such as the three secret weapons to great recruitment, which make a real difference.

Then there's the fact that they often have to dismantle useless or damaging practices and programs that may have existed within their organisation for many years. This can be difficult to do when the very people who built them are now charged with their demolition. Yet it's essential. When Steve Jobs took over as Apple CEO he shrank the company's product development line from 350 to 10 and achieved extraordinary success. He summed up this philosophy later: 'People think focus means saying yes to the thing you've got to focus on. But that's not what it means at all. It means saying no to the hundred other ... ideas that there are. You have to pick carefully. I'm actually as proud of the things we haven't done as the things I have done'.

And it all takes time. I've harped on about speed throughout this book, but this only applies once the fundamentals are in place. The Highfliers 7-step System is no 'quick fix'. It takes about thirty days for actions to become habitual so adopting a slow, sustained roll-out, implementing the steps one at a time and measuring for effectiveness before moving on to the next one, is a much more successful approach.

Yet in all my experience as a director, an HR leader, a business consultant, an adviser and an avid observer, I've found there's one factor more than any other that's the greatest impediment to 'doing'. It's the ultimate decider, the essential linchpin that determines a company's ability to transform its own people practices and achieve extraordinary business results.

The greatest challenge for most employers lies in changing their own ingrained mindset and that of the people in their organisation. Success depends on their ability to modify every single employee's attitude, to convince them of the realities of twenty-first-century recruitment and retention, and to carry everyone with them on the road to innovation. This battle within is the real 'war for talent'. Waging and winning *this* war is what really counts.

Visit www.winningthewarfortalent.com
for more free tools and resources.

Appendix

The Highfliers 7-step System checklist

Here's a checklist you can use to keep track of where you're at when using the Highfliers 7-step System.

Simply check off each step after you've implemented it.

1 The three secret weapons	Sales practices in place	
	Speed: one week to recruit	
	Recruit for attitude systems in place	
2 The bones of recruitment	Positive corporate attitude to recruitment	
	HR champion with access to company leader	
	Skilled, practised, well-paid recruiter/s	
	Business practices in alignment with recruitment outcomes	
	Involvement of line managers in hiring process	
	Effective HR KPI sheet in use	
3 Attracting	Raving fans people practices: • Time and flexibility • Brightness of future • The actual job itself • Inspiration	

(continued)

3 Attracting (cont'd)	Organisational points of difference identified	
	Attractive selection criteria	
	Benefits-led recruitment ads	
	Recruitment marketing effectiveness KPI in place	
	Inspiring careers website: • Employer benefits • Inspirational recruitment vision	
	Employee referral scheme in place	
	Other suitable candidate pools considered	
4 Screening	Identified desired attitudes	
	Identified essential skills and qualifications	
	Identified practical fit criteria	
	Standard CV screening checklist in use	
	Suitable applicants phone interviewed	
	Face-to-face interviews within one week of receiving CV	
5 Interviewing	Inspiring interview venue that creates great impression	
	Good relationship built with candidate	
	Speed applied	
	Inspiring and challenging interview process	
	Standard consistent questions and format	
	Standard tools to sell benefits of organisation	
	Trial close of all applicants	
	Effective selection and management of recruitment agencies	
	Additional effective testing as required	

6 Engaging	Candidate assessment checklist filled out	
	Reference and background checks completed	
	Work experience completed, as required	
	Psycometric and other testing completed, as required	
	Recruiter bias check	
	Gut instinct check	
	An inspiring and personalised job offer made	
	Warm, welcoming success letter and contract	
	Inspiring first contact system	
	Exit interview system in place	
7 Retaining	Monthly one-on-ones in place	
	KPIs in place	
	Incentives linked to KPIs	
	Monthly reward and recognition scheme in place	
	Annual awards night in place	
	L&D core skills programe in place	
	Inspirational speakers/courses in place	
	Team planning workshops in place	
	Clear communication: monthly and annual	
	Ongoing introduction of new perks	

Endnotes

1 PricewaterhouseCoopers 2013, 16th CEO survey.
2 People Practices Inventory 2011, Aon Hewitt 'Best employers in ANZ'.
3 Russell Investment Group 2011, 'Performance data of companies 1997–2011'.
4 Mercer survey of Australia at work 2008, 'What's working', conducted by Mercer Human Resource Consulting, found costs for replacing an employee who turned over ranged from 50–150 per cent of a person's replacement salary. This includes direct expenses such as advertising and agency fees, as well as all the indirect ones such as the price of induction; the charge for the manager and/or recruiter's time; loss of productivity while the new person gets up to speed; and the opportunity costs of having an empty chair when productivity is high. Multiple other qualified sources report the same or even higher percentages.
5 Salt, B 2011, 'Baby boom to baby bust', *Weekend Australian,* 28–9 May.
6 'Signing Up People Ongoing Battle', *The Australian*, 25 November 2006
7 2007, 'Town's $500 000 sign-on offer fails to attract one city doctor', *Australian*, 27 June, p.5.
8 Gajendran, RS & Harrison, DA 2007, 'The good, the bad and the unknown about telecommuting: Meta-Analysis of Psychological Mediators and Individual Consequences', PhD, Pennsylvania State University, in *Journal of Applied Psychology*, vol. 92, no. 6, pp. 1524–41.

9 From 34 & to 63%, Matos K & Galinsky, E 2012, 'National study of employers', Families and Work Institute.

10 Herzberg, F, Mausner, B & Bloch Snyderman, B 1959, *The Motivation to Work*, John Wiley & Sons, New York.

11 Blanchard, K, Bowles S & Mackay, H 1993, *Raving Fans — a revolutionary approach to customer service*, William Morrow & Co, New York.

12 Collins J & Hansen, MT 2011, *Great by Choice: uncertainty, chaos and luck — why some thrive despite them all*, HarperBusiness, New York, ch 4.

13 Rowling, JK 1999, *Harry Potter and the Chamber of Secrets*, Scholastic Inc., p. 333.

14 Lewis, M 2004, *Moneyball*, WW Norton & co., New York, p. 68.

15 Insync Surveys 2012, www.insyncsurveys.com.au.

16 Lewis, M op. cit. p.17.

17 ibid. p. 23.

18 'High impact performance management survey' 2011, Bersin & Associates.

19 Posted by Joris Luijke 16 January 2011, www.managementexchange .com/story/atlassians-big-experiment-performance-reviews.

20 'The growing influence of employee recognition' 2012, Workforce Mood Tracker Survey, Globoforce, Spring.

21 Stolovitch, Clark & Condly 2002, 'Incentives, motivation and workplace performance', The Incentive Research Foundation, Spring.

22 Gottliebsen, R 2003, *10 Best and 10 Worst Decisions of Australian CEOs*, Penguin Books, Australia, p. 256.

23 LeBoeuf, M 1988, *How to Motivate People,* Sidgwick & Jackson Ltd, p. 96.

24 Delta Airlines 2008, RPI best practices recipient, Diamond H Recognition; and Merchiore S 2008, 'Giving recognition a lift', *HR today*, September.

25 Norman, A 2007, 'Avis budget group: using recognition to foster engagement', *workspan* magazine, November.

26 Stuewe, T 2009, Senior Vice President of North American Operations for Sutherland Global Services, paper presented at the Executive Recognition Summit, summarised by Tanner OC.

27 American Society of Training and Development study 2002, quoted by Strother, J, Florida Institute of Technology, in her research paper, 'An assessment of the effectiveness of e-learning in corporate training programmes', April.

28 2013, 'Human resource managers cite lack of communication as main source of low employee morale' survey, Accountemps press release, 22 October.

29 2013, 'Employee confidence survey', Glassdoor, July.

30 In the 'Great place to work' awards 2012, which assessed 2.5 million employees in 45 countries.

31 Weitzner, M & Safer, M 2003, '60 Minutes/SAS: The royal treatment', 20 April.

32 SAS Press release 2012, SAS on *Fortune* magazine's 'Best companies to work for' list, January.

33 Gallup press release 2013, 'Worldwide 13% of employees are engaged at work', 8 October.

34 D5 conference 2007, 'All things digital', 30 May.

Reference list

Bierce, A 2011, *The Devil's Dictionary*, Library of America, New York.

Blanchard, K & Bowles S 1996, *Raving fans: a revolutionary approach to customer service*, Pfeiffer Wiley, New Jersey.

Collins, J 2001, *Good to Great*, Random House, London.

Collins, J & Hansen, MT 2011, *Great by Choice: uncertainty, chaos and luck — why some thrive despite them all*, Harper Business, New York.

Covey, S 1989, *The 7 Habits of Highly Effective People*, Free Press, New York.

Gallo, C 2012, *The Apple Experience: secrets to building insanely great customer loyalty*, McGraw-Hill, Columbus.

Gottliebsen, R 2003, *10 Best and 10 Worst Decisions of Australian CEOs 1992–2002*, Penguin, Victoria.

Herzberg, F, Frederick, M, Bernard, B & Snyderman, B 1959, *The Motivation to Work*, Wiley, New York

Johnson, M 2005, *Family Village Tribe: the story of Flight Centre*, Random House, Sydney.

Le Boeuf, M 1985, *How to Motivate People: reward, the greatest management principle in the world*, Schwartz & Wilkinson, Melbourne.

Lewis, M 2004, *Moneyball*, WW Norton and Co., New York.

Peale, NV 1996, *The Power of Positive Thinking*, Ballantine Books, New York.

Rowling, JK 1998, *Harry Potter and the Chamber of Secrets*, Bloomsbury, London.

Salt, B 2011, *The Big Tilt*, Hardie Grant Books, Richmond.

Walton, S 1992, *Sam Walton: made in America*, Doubleday Dell, New York.

Index

Want to know more?

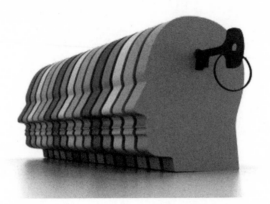

Here are some other resources to help you attract and retain great people

- **Firstly, there's a website with free tools** to help you implement everything you've learned: **www.winningthewarfortalent.com.**

- **Secondly, you can get specific practical help for your organisation by attending one of my 'Winning the War for Talent' master classes.** I also speak and consult about these ideas and practices. Visit the website for details.

- **Finally, if you believe that great people are the heart and soul of every successful organisation, connect with me on the website.** Share the projects that you are implementing and how the book has helped; comment on the awesome, the interesting and the absurd at your workplace; contribute new insights and evidence; or simply subscribe to my e-newsletter for regular updates on my ongoing campaign to change the way organisations practise people strategies.

Learn more with practical advice from our experts

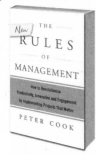

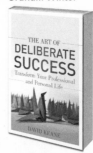